DOVER · THRIFT · EDITIONS

Dark Night of the Soul

ST. JOHN OF THE CROSS

Translated by
E. Allison Peers

from the critical edition of
P. Silverio de Santa Teresa, C.D.

DOVER PUBLICATIONS, INC.
Mineola, New York

DOVER THRIFT EDITIONS

GENERAL EDITOR: PAUL NEGRI
EDITOR OF THIS VOLUME: T. N. R. ROGERS

Bibliographical Note

This Dover edition, first published in 2003, is a republication of *Dark Night of the Soul* from Volume I of the revised (1953) edition of *The Complete Works of Saint John of the Cross, Doctor of the Church*, translated and edited by E. Allison Peers from the critical edition of P. Silverio de Santa Teresa, C. D., which was originally published by The Newman Press, Westminister, Maryland, in 1935. The text is unabridged, but some of Silverio's and Peers's footnotes and the second part of Silverio's introduction have been omitted. We have written a new introductory Note especially for the Dover edition.

Library of Congress Cataloging-in-Publication Data

John of the Cross, Saint, 1542–1591.
 [Noche oscura del alma. English]
 Dark night of the soul / St. John of the Cross ; translated by E. Allison Peers ; from the critical edition of Silverio de Santa Teresa.
  p. cm.
 Originally published: 3rd ed. Westminster, Md. : Newman Press, 1953. With new introd.
 ISBN-13: 978-0-486-42693-8
 ISBN-10: 0-486-42693-9
 1. Mysticism—Catholic Church. I. Peers, E. Allison (Edgar Allison), 1891–1952. II. Silverio, of St. Teresa, 1878–1954. III. Title.

BV5082.3.J6513 2003
248.2'2—dc21   2002041721

Manufactured in the United States by RR Donnelley
42693908   2015
www.doverpublications.com

TO THE

DISCALCED CARMELITES OF CASTILE,

WITH ABIDING MEMORIES OF THEIR HOSPITALITY AND KINDNESS

IN MADRID, AVILA AND BURGOS,

BUT ABOVE ALL OF THEIR DEVOTION TO

SAINT JOHN OF THE CROSS,

I DEDICATE THIS TRANSLATION

Note

JUAN DE YEPES Y ALVAREZ, later to be known as Juan de la Cruz (John of the Cross), was born to an impoverished but love-rich couple in the small town of Fontiveros, Spain on 24 June 1542. His father came from a wealthy family but—after being disowned when he married Catalina Alvarez, a humble weaver—took up his wife's trade. Juan's father died when Juan was only seven, and Catalina was left without even the bare necessities of life for herself and her two sons. Juan became an attendant at a smallpox hospital—whose director, impressed by the boy's compassion, offered to pay for his religious education. Juan studied with the Jesuits and then entered the Carmelite order. He finished his education at the University of Salamanca, where he began teaching while still a student, and was ordained at twenty-five. Soon after, he met Teresa of Avila, a great mystic who took a liking to the young priest and enlisted him in her attempts to reform the Carmelite order. She believed that religious practitioners must embrace poverty, and therefore her branch of the Carmelites became known as "Discalced," or shoeless. Juan first moved to a Discalced nunnery as its confessor, and in 1568 moved to a tiny farmhouse, where he established the first monastery of the reformed Carmelites.

In 1575, however, the traditional Carmelites virtually outlawed the Discalced sect, and two years later they seized Juan and took him to Toledo as their prisoner. When he refused to recant, he was imprisoned in a windowless cell. Three times a week they let him out to eat his daily meal of bread and water, after which he was whipped for his continuing obstinacy. He wrote some of his finest poetry during this imprisonment. After nine months, he broke out by scaling the walls and found refuge with nearby nuns.

His persecution ended in 1578 with the death of the superior general of the traditional Carmelites, and he wrote the majority of his works (most of which remained unfinished) during the next nine years. A few years after Teresa's death (in 1582), the Discalced Carmelites were again troubled by dissension, and Juan was stripped of his offices and forbidden any kind of activity in the order. Juan received this as a blessing because it allowed him to return to a life of solitary contemplation. He died on 14 December 1591 in Ubeda, Spain, and was beatified in 1675, canonized in 1726, and named a doctor of the church in 1926.

Noche obscura del alma (The Dark Night of the Soul), which first appeared at Barcelona in 1619, is probably the best-known work of St. John of the Cross. This great work of Catholic mysticism is an exposition, line by line, of the eight brief stanzas of the poem "Dark Night of the Soul" that he wrote during his imprisonment at Toledo. (*The Ascent of Mount Carmel* is another exposition of the same poem.) The poem seems to have been inspired by the Song of Songs in the Bible, and presents the Christian as a lover passionately seeking divine union with Christ. In his explication of the poem, St. John of the Cross attempts to show that the soul must become emptied of self—purified of the last traces of earthly dross—before it can be filled with God. In this way, the earnest yearner after God may own nothing, but possess everything—the soul's indescribably sublime union with God.

P. SILVERIO DE SANTA TERESA, the editor of the fine critical edition that we have used as the source for this book, wrote the Introduction and most of the footnotes in the text. Footnotes in brackets were added by the translator, E. Allison Peers.

Contents

Introduction

SOMEWHAT reluctantly, out of respect for a venerable tradition, we publish the *Dark Night* as a separate treatise, though in reality it is a continuation of the *Ascent of Mount Carmel* and fulfils the undertakings given in it:

> The first night or purgation is of the sensual part of the soul, which is treated in the present stanza, and will be treated in the first part of this book. And the second is of the spiritual part; of this speaks the second stanza, which follows; and of this we shall treat likewise, in the second and the third part, with respect to the activity of the soul; *and in the fourth part, with respect to its passivity.*[1]

This "fourth part" is the *Dark Night*. Of it the Saint writes in a passage which follows that just quoted:

> And the second night, or purification, pertains to those who are already proficient, occurring at the time when God desires to bring them to the state of union with God. And this latter night is a more obscure and dark and terrible purgation, as we shall say afterwards.

In his three earlier books he has written of the Active Night, of Sense and of Spirit; he now proposes to deal with the Passive Night, in the same order. He has already taught us how we are to deny and purify

---

[1] [*Ascent of Mount Carmel*, Book I, chapter I, section 2.]

ourselves with the ordinary help of grace, in order to prepare our senses and faculties for union with God through love. He now proceeds to explain, with an arresting freshness, how these same senses and faculties are purged and purified by God with a view to the same end—that of union. The combined description of the two nights completes the presentation of active and passive purgation, to which the Saint limits himself in these treatises, although the subject of the stanzas which he is glossing is a much wider one, comprising the whole of the mystical life and ending only with the Divine embraces of the soul transformed in God through love.

The stanzas expounded by the Saint are taken from the same poem in the two treatises. The commentary upon the second, however, is very different from that upon the first, for it assumes a much more advanced state of development. The Active Night has left the senses and faculties well prepared, though not completely prepared, for the reception of Divine influences and illuminations in greater abundance than before. The Saint here postulates a principle of dogmatic theology—that by himself, and with the ordinary aid of grace, man cannot attain to that degree of purgation which is essential to his transformation in God. He needs Divine aid more abundantly. "However greatly the soul itself labours," writes the Saint, "it cannot actively purify itself so as to be in the least degree prepared for the Divine union of perfection of love, if God takes not its hand and purges it not in that dark fire."

The Passive Nights, in which it is God Who accomplishes the purgation, are based upon this incapacity. Souls "begin to enter" this dark night

> when God draws them forth from the state of beginners—which is the state of those that meditate on the spiritual road—and begins to set them in the state of progressives—which is that of those who are already contemplatives—to the end that, after passing through it, they may arrive at the state of the perfect, which is that of the Divine union of the soul with God.

Before explaining the nature and effects of this Passive Night, the Saint touches, in passing, upon certain imperfections found in those who are about to enter it and which it removes by the process of purgation. Such travellers are still untried proficients, who have not yet acquired mature habits of spirituality and who therefore still conduct themselves as children. The imperfections are examined one by one, following the order of the seven deadly sins, in chapters (II–VIII) which once more reveal the author's skill as a director of souls. They are easy chapters to understand, and of great practical utility, comparable to those in the first book of the *Ascent* which deal with the active purgation of the desires of sense.

In Chapter VIII, St. John of the Cross begins to describe the Passive Night of the senses, the principal aim of which is the purgation or stripping of the soul of its imperfections and the preparation of it for fruitive union. The Passive Night of Sense, we are told, is "common" and "comes to many," whereas that of Spirit "is the portion of very few." The one is "bitter and terrible" but "the second bears no comparison with it," for it is "horrible and awful to the spirit." A good deal of literature on the former Night existed in the time of St. John of the Cross and he therefore promises to be brief in his treatment of it. Of the latter, on the other hand, he will "treat more fully . . . since very little has been said of this, either in speech or in writing, and very little is known of it, even by experience."

Having described this Passive Night of Sense in Chapter VIII, he explains with great insight and discernment how it may be recognized whether any given aridity is a result of this Night or whether it comes from sins or imperfections, or from frailty or lukewarmness of spirit, or even from indisposition or "humours" of the body. The Saint is particularly effective here, and we may once more compare this chapter with a similar one in the *Ascent* (II, XIII) — that in which he fixes the point where the soul may abandon discursive meditation and enter the contemplation which belongs to loving and simple faith.

Both these chapters have contributed to the reputation of St. John of the Cross as a consummate spiritual master. And this not only for the objective value of his observations, but because, even in spite of himself, he betrays the sublimity of his own mystical experiences. Once more, too, we may admire the crystalline transparency of his teaching and the precision of the phrases in which he clothes it. To judge by his language alone, one might suppose at times that he is speaking of mathematical, rather than of spiritual operations.

In Chapter X, the Saint describes the discipline which the soul in this Dark Night must impose upon itself; this, as might be logically deduced from the *Ascent*, consists in "allowing the soul to remain in peace and quietness," content "with a peaceful and loving attentiveness toward God." Before long it will experience enkindlings of love (Chapter XI), which will serve to purify its sins and imperfections and draw it gradually nearer to God; we have here, as it were, so many stages of the ascent of the Mount on whose summit the soul attains to transforming union. Chapters XII and XIII detail with great exactness the benefits that the soul receives from this aridity, while Chapter XIV

briefly expounds the last line of the first stanza and brings to an end
what the Saint desires to say with respect to the first Passive Night.

At only slightly greater length St. John of the Cross describes the
Passive Night of the Spirit, which is at once more afflictive and more
painful than those which have preceded it. This, nevertheless, is the
Dark Night *par excellence,* of which the Saint speaks in these words:
"The night which we have called that of sense may and should be
called a kind of correction and restraint of the desire rather than
purgation. The reason is that all the imperfections and disorders of the
sensual part have their strength and root in the spirit, where all habits,
both good and bad, are brought into subjection, and thus, until these
are purged, the rebellions and depravities of sense cannot be purged
thoroughly."

Spiritual persons, we are told, do not enter the second night immediately after leaving the first; on the contrary, they generally pass a long
time, even years, before doing so, for they still have many imperfections, both habitual and actual (Chapter II). After a brief introduction
(Chapter III), the Saint describes with some fullness the nature of this
spiritual purgation or dark contemplation referred to in the first stanza
of his poem and the varieties of pain and affliction caused by it,
whether in the soul or in its faculties (Chapters IV–VIII). These chapters
are brilliant beyond all description; in them we seem to reach the cul-
minating point of their author's mystical experience; any excerpt from
them would do them an injustice. It must suffice to say that St. John of
the Cross seldom again touches those same heights of sublimity.

Chapter IX describes how, although these purgations seem to blind
the spirit, they do so only to enlighten it again with a brighter and
intenser light, which it is preparing itself to receive with greater abundance. The following chapter makes the comparison between spiritual
purgation and the log of wood which gradually becomes transformed
through being immersed in fire and at last takes on the fire's own properties. The force with which the familiar similitude is driven home
impresses indelibly upon the mind the fundamental concept of this
most sublime of all purgations. Marvellous, indeed, are its effects, from
the first enkindlings and burnings of Divine love, which are greater
beyond comparison than those produced by the Night of Sense, the one
being as different from the other as is the body from the soul. "For this
(latter) is an enkindling of spiritual love in the soul, which, in the midst
of these dark confines, feels itself to be keenly and sharply wounded in
strong Divine love, and to have a certain realization and foretaste of
God." No less wonderful are the effects of the powerful Divine illumination which from time to time enfolds the soul in the splendours of

glory. When the effects of the light that wounds and yet illumines are combined with those of the enkindlement that melts the soul with its heat, the delights experienced are so great as to be ineffable.

The second line of the first stanza of the poem is expounded in three admirable chapters (XI-XIII), while one short chapter (XIV) suffices for the three lines remaining. We then embark upon the second stanza, which describes the soul's security in the Dark Night—due, among other reasons, to its being freed "not only from itself, but likewise from its other enemies, which are the world and the devil."

This contemplation is not only dark, but also secret (Chapter XVII), and in Chapter XVIII is compared to the "staircase" of the poem. This comparison suggests to the Saint an exposition (Chapters XVIII, XIX) of the ten steps or degrees of love which comprise St. Bernard's mystical ladder. Chapter XXI describes the soul's "disguise," from which the book passes on (Chapters XXII, XXIII) to extol the "happy chance" which led it to journey "in darkness and concealment" from its enemies, both without and within.

Chapter XXIV glosses the last line of the second stanza—"my house being now at rest." Both the higher and the lower "portions of the soul" are now tranquilized and prepared for the desired union with the Spouse, a union which is the subject that the Saint proposed to treat in his commentary on the five remaining stanzas. As far as we know, this commentary was never written. We have only the briefest outline of what was to have been covered in the third, in which, following the same effective metaphor of night, the Saint describes the excellent properties of the spiritual night of infused contemplation, through which the soul journeys with no other guide or support, either outward or inward, than the Divine love "which burned in my heart."

It is difficult to express adequately the sense of loss that one feels at the premature truncation of this eloquent treatise. We have already given our opinion[2] upon the commentaries thought to have been written on the final stanzas of the "Dark Night." Did we possess them, they would explain the birth of the light—"dawn's first breathings in the heav'ns above"—which breaks through the black darkness of the Active and the Passive Nights; they would tell us, too, of the soul's further progress towards the Sun's full brightness. It is true, of course, that some part of this great gap is filled by St. John of the Cross himself in his other treatises, but it is small compensation for the incomplete state in which he left this edifice of such gigantic proportions that he should

---

[2] [In his introduction to *Ascent of Mount Carmel*.]

have given us other and smaller buildings of a somewhat similar kind. Admirable as are the *Spiritual Canticle* and the *Living Flame of Love*, they are not so completely knit into one whole as is this great double treatise. They lose both in flexibility and in substance through the closeness with which they follow the stanzas of which they are the exposition. In the *Ascent* and the *Dark Night*, on the other hand, we catch only the echoes of the poem, which are all but lost in the resonance of the philosopher's voice and the eloquent tones of the preacher. Nor have the other treatises the learning and the authority of these. Nowhere else does the genius of St. John of the Cross for infusing philosophy into his mystical dissertations find such an outlet as here. Nowhere else, again, is he quite so appealingly human; for, though he is human even in his loftiest and sublimest passages, this intermingling of philosophy with mystical theology makes him seem particularly so. These treatises are a wonderful illustration of the theological truth that grace, far from destroying nature, ennobles and dignifies it, and of the agreement always found between the natural and the supernatural—between the principles of sound reason and the sublimest manifestations of Divine grace.

P. Silverio de Santa Teresa, c.d.

Dark Night of the Soul

DARK NIGHT

Exposition of the stanzas describing the method followed by the soul in its journey upon the spiritual road to the attainment of the perfect union of love with God, to the extent that is possible in this life. Likewise are described the properties belonging to the soul that has attained to the said perfection, according as they are contained in the same stanzas.

PROLOGUE

IN THIS book are first set down all the stanzas which are to be expounded; afterwards, each of the stanzas is expounded separately, being set down before its exposition; and then each line is expounded separately and in turn, the line itself also being set down before the exposition. In the first two stanzas are expounded the effects of the two spiritual purgations: of the sensual part of man and of the spiritual part. In the other six are expounded various and wondrous effects of the spiritual illumination and union of love with God.

STANZAS OF THE SOUL

1. On a dark night, Kindled in love with yearnings—oh, happy chance!—
   I went forth without being observed, My house being now at rest.

2. In darkness and secure, By the secret ladder, disguised—oh, happy chance!—
   In darkness and in concealment, My house being now at rest.

3. In the happy night, In secret, when none saw me,

Nor I beheld aught,   Without light or guide, save that which burned
in my heart.

4. This light guided me   More surely than the light of noonday
To the place where he (well I knew who!) was awaiting me—   A place
where none appeared.

5. Oh, night that guided me,   Oh, night more lovely than the dawn,
Oh, night that joined Beloved with lover,   Lover transformed in the
Beloved!

6. Upon my flowery breast,   Kept wholly for himself alone,
There he stayed sleeping, and I caressed him,   And the fanning of
the cedars made a breeze.

7. The breeze blew from the turret   As I parted his locks;
With his gentle hand he wounded my neck   And caused all my
senses to be suspended.

8. I remained, lost in oblivion;   My face I reclined on the Beloved.
All ceased and I abandoned myself,   Leaving my cares forgotten
among the lilies.

Begins the exposition of the stanzas which treat of the way and manner
which the soul follows upon the road of the union of love with God.

Before we enter upon the exposition of these stanzas, it is well to understand here that the soul that utters them is now in the state of perfection,
which is the union of love with God, having already passed through severe
trials and straits, by means of spiritual exercise in the narrow way of eternal life whereof Our Saviour speaks in the Gospel, along which way the
soul ordinarily passes in order to reach this high and happy union with
God. Since this road (as the Lord Himself says likewise) is so strait, and
since there are so few that enter by it,[1] the soul considers it a great happiness and good chance to have passed along it to the said perfection of love,
as it sings in this first stanza, calling this strait road with full propriety "dark
night," as will be explained hereafter in the lines of the said stanza. The
soul, then, rejoicing at having passed along this narrow road whence so
many blessings have come to it, speaks after this manner.

---

[1] St. Matthew vii, 14.

BOOK THE FIRST

Which treats of the Night of Sense.

On a dark night, Kindled in love with yearnings—oh, happy chance!—
I went forth without being observed, My house being now at rest.

EXPOSITION

IN THIS first stanza the soul relates the way and manner which it followed in going forth, as to its affection, from itself and from all things, and in dying to them all and to itself, by means of true mortification, in order to attain to living the sweet and delectable life of love with God; and it says that this going forth from itself and from all things was a "dark night," by which, as will be explained hereafter, is here understood purgative contemplation, which causes passively in the soul the negation of itself and of all things referred to above.

2. And this going forth it says here that it was able to accomplish in the strength and ardour which love for its Spouse gave to it for that purpose in the dark contemplation aforementioned. Herein it extols the great happiness which it found in journeying to God through this night with such signal success that none of the three enemies, which are world, devil and flesh (who are they that ever impede this road), could hinder it; inasmuch as the aforementioned night of purgative contemplation lulled to sleep and mortified, in the house of its sensuality, all the passions and desires with respect to their mischievous desires and motions.

The line, then, says:

On a dark night.

3

CHAPTER I

Sets down the first line and begins to treat of the imperfections of beginners.

INTO THIS dark night souls begin to enter when God draws them forth from the state of beginners—which is the state of those that meditate on the spiritual road—and begins to set them in the state of progressives—which is that of those who are already contemplatives—to the end that, after passing through it, they may arrive at the state of the perfect, which is that of the Divine union of the soul with God. Wherefore, to the end that we may the better understand and explain what night is this through which the soul passes, and for what cause God sets it therein, it will be well here to touch first of all upon certain characteristics of beginners (which, although we treat them with all possible brevity, will not fail to be of service likewise to the beginners themselves), in order that, realizing the weakness of the state wherein they are, they may take courage, and may desire that God will bring them into this night, wherein the soul is strengthened and confirmed in the virtues, and made ready for the inestimable delights of the love of God. And, although we may tarry here for a time, it will not be for longer than is necessary, so that we may go on to speak at once of this dark night.

2. It must be known, then, that the soul, after it has been definitely converted to the service of God, is, as a rule, spiritually nurtured and caressed by God, even as is the tender child by its loving mother, who warms it with the heat of her bosom and nurtures it with sweet milk and soft and pleasant food, and carries it and caresses it in her arms; but, as the child grows bigger, the mother gradually ceases caressing it, and, hiding her tender love, puts bitter aloes upon her sweet breast, sets down the child from her arms and makes it walk upon its feet, so that it may lose the habits of a child and betake itself to more important and substantial occupations. The loving mother is like the grace of God, for, as soon as

4

the soul is regenerated by its new warmth and fervour for the service of God, He treats it in the same way; He makes it to find spiritual milk, sweet and delectable, in all the things of God, without any labor of its own, and also great pleasure in spiritual exercises, for here God is giving to it the breast of His tender love, even as to a tender child.

3. Therefore, such a soul finds its delight in spending long periods — perchance whole nights — in prayer; penances are its pleasures; fasts its joys; and its consolations are to make use of the sacraments and to occupy itself in Divine things. In the which things spiritual persons (though taking part in them with great efficacy and persistence and using and treating them with great care) often find themselves, spiritually speaking, very weak and imperfect. For since they are moved to these things and to these spiritual exercises by the consolation and pleasure that they find in them, and since, too, they have not been prepared for them by the practice of earnest striving in the virtues, they have many faults and imperfections with respect to these spiritual actions of theirs; for, after all, any man's actions correspond to the habit of perfection attained by him. And, as these persons have not had the opportunity of acquiring the said habits of strength, they have necessarily to work like feeble children, feebly. In order that this may be seen more clearly, and likewise how much these beginners in the virtues lack with respect to the works in which they so readily engage with the pleasure aforementioned, we shall describe it by reference to the seven capital sins, each in its turn, indicating some of the many imperfections which they have under each heading; wherein it will be clearly seen how like to children are these persons in all they do. And it will also be seen how many blessings the dark night of which we shall afterwards treat brings with it, since it cleanses the soul and purifies it from all these imperfections.

CHAPTER II Pride

Of certain spiritual imperfections which beginners have with respect to the habit of pride.

AS THESE beginners feel themselves to be very fervent and diligent in spiritual things and devout exercises, from this prosperity (although it is true that holy things of their own nature cause humility) there often comes to them, through their imperfections, a certain kind of secret pride, whence they come to have some degree of satisfaction with their works and with themselves. And hence there comes to them likewise a certain desire, which is somewhat vain, and at times very vain, to speak of spiritual things in the presence of others, and sometimes even to teach such things rather than to learn them. They condemn others in their heart when they see that they have not the kind of devotion which they themselves desire; and sometimes they even say this in words, herein resembling the Pharisee, who boasted of himself, praising God for his own good works and despising the publican.[1]

2. In these persons the devil often increases the fervour that they have and the desire to perform these and other works more frequently, so that their pride and presumption may grow greater. For the devil knows quite well that all these works and virtues which they perform are not only valueless to them, but even become vices in them. And such a degree of evil are some of these persons wont to reach that they would have none appear good save themselves; and thus, in deed and word, whenever the opportunity occurs, they condemn them and slander them, beholding the mote in their brother's eye and not considering the beam which is in their own;[2] they strain at another's gnat and themselves swallow a camel.[3]

3. Sometimes, too, when their spiritual masters, such as confessors and superiors, do not approve of their spirit and behavior (for they are anxious that all they do shall be esteemed and praised), they consider that they do not understand them, or that, because they do not approve of this and comply with that, their confessors are themselves not spiritual. And so they immediately desire and contrive to find some one else who will fit in with their tastes; for as a rule they desire to speak of spiritual matters with those who they think will praise and esteem what they do, and they flee, as they would from death, from those who disabuse them in order to lead them into a safe road—sometimes they even harbour ill-will against them. Presuming thus, they are wont to resolve much and accomplish very little. Sometimes they are anxious that others shall realize how spiritual and devout they are, to which end they occasionally give outward evidence thereof in movements, sighs and other ceremonies; and at times they are apt to fall into certain ecstasies, in public rather than in secret, wherein the devil aids them, and they are pleased that this should be noticed, and are often eager that it should be noticed more.

4. Many such persons desire to be the favorites of their confessors and to become intimate with them, as a result of which there beset

---

[1] St. Luke xviii, 11–12.
[2] St. Matthew vii, 3.
[3] St. Matthew xxiii, 24.

them continual occasions of envy and disquiet. They are too much embarrassed to confess their sins nakedly, lest their confessors should think less of them, so they palliate them and make them appear less evil, and thus it is to excuse themselves rather than to accuse themselves that they go to confession. And sometimes they seek another confessor to tell the wrongs that they have done, so that their own confessor shall think they have done nothing wrong at all, but only good; and thus they always take pleasure in telling him what is good, and sometimes in such terms as make it appear to be greater than it is rather than less, desiring that he may think them to be good, when it would be greater humility in them, as we shall say, to depreciate it, and to desire that neither he nor anyone else should consider them of account.

5. Some of these beginners, too, make little of their faults, and at other times become over-sad when they see themselves fall into them, thinking themselves to have been saints already; and thus they become angry and impatient with themselves, which is another imperfection. Often they beseech God, with great yearnings, that He will take from them their imperfections and faults, but they do this that they may find themselves at peace, and may not be troubled by them, rather than for God's sake; not realizing that, if He should take their imperfections from them, they would probably become prouder and more presumptuous still. They dislike praising others and love to be praised themselves; sometimes they seek out such praise. Herein they are like the foolish virgins, who, when their lamps could not be lit, sought oil from others.[4]

6. From these imperfections some souls go on to develop many very grave ones, which do them great harm. But some have fewer and some more, and some, only the first motions thereof or little beyond these; and there are hardly any such beginners who, at the time of these signs of fervour, fall not into some of these errors. But those who at this time are going on to perfection proceed very differently and with quite another temper of spirit; for they progress by means of humility and are greatly edified, not only thinking naught of their own affairs, but having very little satisfaction with themselves; they consider all others as far better, and usually have a holy envy of them, and an eagerness to serve God as they do. For the greater is their fervour, and the more numerous are the works that they perform, and the greater is the pleasure that they take in them, as they progress in humility, the more do they realize how much God deserves of them, and how little is all that they do for His sake; and thus,

---

[4] St. Matthew xxv, 8. [*Lit.*, "who, having their lamps dead, sought oil from without."]

the more they do, the less are they satisfied. So much would they gladly
do from charity and love for Him, that all they do seems to them naught;
and so greatly are they importuned, occupied and absorbed by this loving
anxiety that they never notice what others do or do not; or if they do notice
it, they always believe, as I say, that all others are far better than they themselves. Wherefore, holding themselves as of little worth, they are anxious
that others too should thus hold them, and should despise and depreciate
that which they do. And further, if men should praise and esteem them,
they can in no wise believe what they say; it seems to them strange that
anyone should say these good things of them.

7. Together with great tranquillity and humbleness, these souls have
a deep desire to be taught by anyone who can bring them profit; they
are the complete opposite of those of whom we have spoken above,
who would fain be always teaching, and who, when others seem to be
teaching them, take the words from their mouths as if they knew them
already. These souls, on the other hand, being far from desiring to be
the masters of any, are very ready to travel and set out on another road
than that which they are actually following, if they be so commanded,
because they never think that they are right in anything whatsoever.
They rejoice when others are praised; they grieve only because they
serve not God like them. They have no desire to speak of the things that
they do, because they think so little of them that they are ashamed to
speak of them even to their spiritual masters, since they seem to them
to be things that merit not being spoken of. They are more anxious to
speak of their faults and sins, or that these should be recognized rather
than their virtues; and thus they incline to talk of their souls with those
who account their actions and their spirituality of little value. This is a
characteristic of the spirit which is simple, pure, genuine and very
pleasing to God. For as the wise Spirit of God dwells in these humble
souls, He moves them and inclines them to keep His treasures secretly
within and likewise to cast out from themselves all evil. God gives this
grace to the humble, together with the other virtues, even as He denies
it to the proud.

8. These souls will give their heart's blood to anyone that serves God,
and will help others to serve Him as much as in them lies. The imperfections into which they see themselves fall they bear with humility,
meekness of spirit and a loving fear of God, hoping in Him. But souls
who in the beginning journey with this kind of perfection are, as I
understand, and as has been said, a minority, and very few are those
who we can be glad do not fall into the opposite errors. For this reason,
as we shall afterwards say, God leads into the dark night those whom
He desires to purify from all these imperfections so that He may bring
them farther onward.

CHAPTER III   *Avarice*

Of some imperfections which some of these souls are apt to have, with respect to the second capital sin, which is avarice, in the spiritual sense.

MANY OF these beginners have also at times great spiritual avarice. They will be found to be discontented with the spirituality which God gives them; and they are very disconsolate and querulous because they find not in spiritual things the consolation that they would desire. Many can never have enough of listening to counsels and learning spiritual precepts, and of possessing and reading many books which treat of this matter, and they spend their time on all these things rather than on works of mortification and the perfecting of the inward poverty of spirit which should be theirs. Furthermore, they burden themselves with images and rosaries which are very curious; now they put down one, now take up another; now they change about, now change back again; now they want this kind of thing, now that, preferring one kind of cross to another, because it is more curious. And others you will see adorned with agnus-deis[1] and relics and tokens,[2] like children with trinkets. Here I condemn the attachment of the heart, and the affection which they have for the nature, multitude and curiosity of these things, inasmuch as it is quite contrary to poverty of spirit, which considers only the substance of devotion, makes use only of what suffices for that end and grows weary of this other kind of multiplicity and curiosity. For true devotion must issue from the heart, and consists in the truth and substance alone of what is represented by spiritual things; all the rest is affection and attachment proceeding from imperfection; and in order that one may pass to any kind of perfection it is necessary for such desires to be killed.

2. I knew a person who for more than ten years made use of a cross roughly formed from a branch[3] that had been blessed, fastened with a pin twisted round it; he had never ceased using it, and he always carried it about with him until I took it from him; and this was a person of no small sense and understanding. And I saw another who said his

---

[1] The *agnusdei* was a wax medal with a representation of the Lamb stamped upon it, often blessed by the Pope; at the time of the Saint such medals were greatly sought after, as we know from various references in St. Teresa's letters.

[2] [The word *nómina*, translated "token," and normally meaning "list" or "roll," refers to a relic on which were written the names of saints. In modern Spanish it can denote a medal or amulet used superstitiously.]

[3] [No doubt a branch of palm, olive, or rosemary, blessed in church on Palm Sunday, like the English palm crosses of today. "Palm Sunday" is in Spanish *Domingo de ramos*: "Branch Sunday."]

prayers using beads that were made of bones from the spine of a fish; his devotion was certainly no less precious on that account in the sight of God, for it is clear that these things carried no devotion in their workmanship or value. Those, then, who start from these beginnings and make good progress attach themselves to no visible instruments, nor do they burden themselves with such, nor desire to know more than is necessary in order that they may act well; for they set their eyes only on being right with God and on pleasing Him, and therein consists their covetousness. And thus with great generosity they give away all that they have, and delight to know that they have it not, for God's sake and for charity to their neighbor, no matter whether these be spiritual things or temporal. For, as I say, they set their eyes only upon the reality of interior perfection, which is to give pleasure to God and in naught to give pleasure to themselves.

3. But neither from these imperfections nor from those others can the soul be perfectly purified until God brings it into the passive purgation of that dark night whereof we shall speak presently. It befits the soul, however, to contrive to labor, in so far as it can, on its own account, to the end that it may purge and perfect itself, and thus may merit being taken by God into that Divine care wherein it becomes healed of all things that it was unable of itself to cure. Because, however greatly the soul itself labors, it cannot actively purify itself so as to be in the least degree prepared for the Divine union of perfection of love, if God takes not its hand and purges it not in that dark fire, in the way and manner that we have to describe.

CHAPTER IV *Luxury*

Of other imperfections which these beginners are apt to have with respect to the third sin, which is luxury.

MANY of these beginners have many other imperfections than those which I am describing with respect to each of the deadly sins, but these I set aside, in order to avoid prolixity, touching upon a few of the most important, which are, as it were, the origin and cause of the rest. And thus, with respect to this sin of luxury (leaving apart the falling of spiritual persons into this sin, since my intent is to treat of the imperfections which have to be purged by the dark night), they have many imperfections which might be described as spiritual luxury, not because they are so, but because the imperfections proceed from spiritual things. For it often comes to pass that, in their very spiritual exercises, when they are powerless to prevent it, there arise and assert themselves in the sensual part of the soul impure acts and motions, and sometimes this happens even when the spirit is deep in prayer, or engaged in the Sacrament of Penance or in the Eucharist. These things are not, as I say, in their power; they proceed from one of three causes.

2. The first cause from which they often proceed is the pleasure which human nature takes in spiritual things. For when the spirit and the sense are pleased, every part of a man is moved by that pleasure to delight according to its proportion and nature. For then the spirit, which is the higher part, is moved to pleasure and delight in God; and the sensual nature, which is the lower part, is moved to pleasure and delight of the senses, because it cannot possess and lay hold upon aught else, and it therefore lays hold upon that which comes nearest to itself, which is the impure and sensual. Thus it comes to pass that the soul is in deep prayer with God according to the spirit, and, on the other hand, according to sense it is passively conscious, not without great displeasure, of rebellions and motions and acts of the senses, which often happens in Communion, for when the soul receives joy and comfort in this act of love, because this Lord bestows it (since it is to that end that He gives Himself), the sensual nature takes that which is its own likewise, as we have said, after its manner. Now as, after all, these two parts are combined in one individual, they ordinarily both participate in that which one of them receives, each after its manner; for, as the philosopher says, everything that is received is in the recipient after the manner of the same recipient. And thus, in these beginnings, and even when the soul has made some progress, its sensual part, being imperfect, oftentimes receives the Spirit of God with the same imperfection. Now when this sensual part is renewed by the purgation of the dark night which we shall describe, it no longer has these weaknesses; for it is no longer this part that receives aught, but rather it is itself received into the Spirit. And thus it then has everything after the manner of the Spirit.

3. The second cause whence these rebellions sometimes proceed is the devil, who, in order to disquiet and disturb the soul, at times when it is at prayer or is striving to pray, contrives to stir up these motions of impurity in its nature; and if the soul gives heed to any of these, they cause it great harm. For through fear of these not only do persons become lax in prayer—which is the aim of the devil when he begins to strive with them—but some give up prayer altogether, because they think that these things attack them more during that exercise than apart from it, which is true, since the devil attacks them then more than at other times, so that they may give up spiritual exercises. And not only so, but he succeeds in portraying to them very vividly things that are most foul and impure, and at times are very closely related to certain

spiritual things and persons that are of profit to their souls, in order to terrify them and make them fearful; so that those who are affected by this dare not even look at anything or meditate upon anything, because they immediately encounter this temptation. And upon those who are inclined to melancholy this acts with such effect that they become greatly to be pitied since they are suffering so sadly; for this trial reaches such a point in certain persons, when they have this evil humour, that they believe it to be clear that the devil is ever present with them and that they have no power to prevent this, although some of these persons can prevent his attack by dint of great effort and labor. When these impurities attack such souls through the medium of melancholy, they are not as a rule freed from them until they have been cured of that kind of humor, unless the dark night has entered the soul, and rids them of all impurities, one after another.

4. The third source whence these impure motions are apt to proceed in order to make war upon the soul is often the fear which such persons have conceived for these impure representations and motions. Something that they see or say or think brings them to their mind, and this makes them afraid, so that they suffer from them through no fault of their own.

5. There are also certain souls of so tender and frail a nature that, when there comes to them some spiritual consolation or some grace in prayer, the spirit of luxury is with them immediately, inebriating and delighting their sensual nature in such manner that it is as if they were plunged into the enjoyment and pleasure of this sin; and the enjoyment remains, together with the consolation, passively, and sometimes they are able to see that certain impure and unruly acts have taken place. The reason for this is that, since these natures are, as I say, frail and tender, their humors are stirred up and their blood is excited at the least disturbance. And hence come these motions; and the same thing happens to such souls when they are enkindled with anger or suffer any disturbance or grief.[1]

6. Sometimes, again, there arises within these spiritual persons, whether

---

[1] All writers who comment upon this delicate matter go into lengthy and learned explanations of it, though in reality there is little that needs to be added to the Saint's clear and apt exposition. It will be remembered that St. Teresa once wrote to her brother Lorenzo, who suffered in this way: "As to those stirrings of sense. . . . I am quite clear they are of no account, so the best thing is to make no account of them" (*The Letters of Saint Teresa of Jesus*, translated and edited by E. Allison Peers, 168). The most effective means of calming souls tormented by these favors is to commend them to a discreet and wise director whose counsel they may safely follow. The Illuminists committed the grossest errors in dealing with this matter.

they be speaking or performing spiritual actions, a certain vigour and bravado, through their having regard to persons who are present, and before these persons they display a certain kind of vain gratification. This also arises from luxury of spirit, after the manner wherein we here understand it, which is accompanied as a rule by complacency in the will.

7. Some of these persons make friendships of a spiritual kind with others, which oftentimes arise from luxury and not from spirituality; this may be known to be the case when the remembrance of that friendship causes not the remembrance and love of God to grow, but occasions remorse of conscience. For, when the friendship is purely spiritual, the love of God grows with it; and the more the soul remembers it, the more it remembers the love of God, and the greater the desire it has for God; so that, as the one grows, the other grows also. For the spirit of God has this property, that it increases good by adding to it more good, inasmuch as there is likeness and conformity between them. But, when this love arises from the vice of sensuality aforementioned, it produces the contrary effects; for the more the one grows, the more the other decreases, and the remembrance of it likewise. If that sensual love grows, it will at once be observed that the soul's love of God is becoming colder, and that it is forgetting Him as it remembers that love; there comes to it, too, a certain remorse of conscience. And, on the other hand, if the love of God grows in the soul, that other love becomes cold and is forgotten; for, as the two are contrary to one another, not only does the one not aid the other, but the one which predominates quenches and confounds the other, and becomes strengthened in itself, as the philosophers say. Wherefore Our Saviour said in the Gospel: "That which is born of the flesh is flesh, and that which is born of the Spirit is spirit."[2] That is to say, the love which is born of sensuality ends in sensuality, and that which is of the spirit ends in the spirit of God and causes it to grow. This is the difference that exists between these two kinds of love, whereby we may know them.

8. When the soul enters the dark night, it brings these kinds of love under control. It strengthens and purifies the one, namely that which is according to God; and the other it removes and brings to an end; and in the beginning it causes both to be lost sight of, as we shall say hereafter.

---

[2] St. John iii, 6.

CHAPTER V   *Wrath*

Of the imperfections into which beginners fall with respect to the sin of wrath.

BY REASON of the concupiscence which many beginners have for spiritual consolations, their experience of these consolations is very commonly accompanied by many imperfections proceeding from the sin of wrath; for, when their delight and pleasure in spiritual things come to an end, they naturally become embittered, and bear that lack of sweetness which they have to suffer with a bad grace, which affects all that they do; and they very easily become irritated over the smallest matter—sometimes, indeed, none can tolerate them. This frequently happens after they have been very pleasantly recollected in prayer according to sense; when their pleasure and delight therein come to an end, their nature is naturally vexed and disappointed, just as is the child when they take it from the breast of which it was enjoying the sweetness. There is no sin in this natural vexation, when it is not permitted to indulge itself, but only imperfection, which must be purged by the aridity and severity of the dark night.

2. There are other of these spiritual persons, again, who fall into another kind of spiritual wrath: this happens when they become irritated at the sins of others, and keep watch on those others with a sort of uneasy zeal. At times the impulse comes to them to reprove them angrily, and occasionally they go so far as to indulge it and set themselves up as masters of virtue. All this is contrary to spiritual meekness.

3. There are others who are vexed with themselves when they observe their own imperfectness, and display an impatience that is not humility; so impatient are they about this that they would fain be saints in a day. Many of these persons purpose to accomplish a great deal and make grand resolutions; yet, as they are not humble and have no misgivings about themselves, the more resolutions they make, the greater is their fall and the greater their annoyance, since they have not the patience to wait for that which God will give them when it pleases Him; this likewise is contrary to the spiritual meekness aforementioned, which cannot be wholly remedied save by the purgation of the dark night. Some souls, on the other hand, are so patient as regards the progress which they desire that God would gladly see them less so.

CHAPTER VI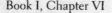

Of imperfections with respect to spiritual gluttony.

WITH RESPECT to the fourth sin, which is spiritual gluttony, there is much to be said, for there is scarce one of these beginners who, however satisfactory his progress, falls not into some of the many imperfections which come to these beginners with respect to this sin, on account of the sweetness which they find at first in spiritual exercises. For many of these, lured by the sweetness and pleasure which they find in such exercises, strive more after spiritual sweetness than after spiritual purity and discretion, which is that which God regards and accepts throughout the spiritual journey. Therefore, besides the imperfections into which the seeking for sweetness of this kind makes them fall, the gluttony which they now have makes them continually go to extremes, so that they pass beyond the limits of moderation within which the virtues are acquired and wherein they have their being. For some of these persons, attracted by the pleasure which they find therein, kill themselves with penances, and others weaken themselves with fasts, by performing more than their frailty can bear, without the order or advice of any, but rather endeavouring to avoid those whom they should obey in these matters; some, indeed, dare to do these things even though the contrary has been commanded them.

2. These persons are most imperfect and unreasonable; for they set bodily penance before subjection and obedience, which is penance according to reason and discretion, and therefore a sacrifice more acceptable and pleasing to God than any other. But such one-sided penance is no more than the penance of beasts, to which they are attracted, exactly like beasts, by the desire and pleasure which they find therein. Inasmuch as all extremes are vicious, and as in behaving thus such persons are working their own will, they grow in vice rather than in virtue; for, to say the least, they are acquiring spiritual gluttony and pride in this way, through not walking in obedience. And many of these the devil assails, stirring up this gluttony in them through the pleasures and desires which he increases within them, to such an extent that, since they can no longer help themselves, they either change or vary or add to that which is commanded them, as any obedience in this respect is so bitter to them. To such an evil pass have some persons come that, simply because it is through obedience that they engage in these

exercises, they lose the desire and devotion to perform them, their only desire and pleasure being to do what they themselves are inclined to do, so that it would probably be more profitable for them not to engage in these exercises at all.

3. You will find that many of these persons are very insistent with their spiritual masters to be granted that which they desire, extracting it from them almost by force; if they be refused it they become as peevish as children and go about in great displeasure, thinking that they are not serving God when they are not allowed to do that which they would. For they go about clinging to their own will and pleasure, which they treat as though it came from God; and immediately their directors take it from them, and try to subject them to the will of God, they become peevish, grow faint-hearted and fall away. These persons think that their own satisfaction and pleasure are the satisfaction and service of God.

4. There are others, again, who, because of this gluttony, know so little of their own unworthiness and misery and have thrust so far from them the loving fear and reverence which they owe to the greatness of God, that they hesitate not to insist continually that their confessors shall allow them to communicate often. And, what is worse, they frequently dare to communicate without the leave and consent of the minister and steward of Christ, merely acting on their own opinion, and contriving to conceal the truth from him. And for this reason, because they desire to communicate continually, they make their confessions carelessly, being more eager to eat than to eat cleanly and perfectly, although it would be healthier and holier for them had they the contrary inclination and begged their confessors not to command them to approach the altar so frequently: between these two extremes, however, the better way is that of humble resignation. But the boldness referred to is a thing that does great harm, and men may fear to be punished for such temerity.

5. These persons, in communicating, strive with every nerve to obtain some kind of sensible sweetness and pleasure, instead of humbly doing reverence and giving praise within themselves to God. And in such wise do they devote themselves to this that, when they have received no pleasure or sweetness in the senses, they think that they have accomplished nothing at all. This is to judge God very unworthily; they have not realized that the least of the benefits which come from this Most Holy Sacrament is that which concerns the senses; and that the invisible part of the grace that it bestows is much greater; for, in order that they may look at it with the eyes of faith, God oftentimes withholds from them these other consolations and sweetnesses of sense. And thus they desire to feel and taste God as though He were comprehensible by

them and accessible to them, not only in this, but likewise in other spiritual practices. All this is very great imperfection and completely opposed to the nature of God, since it is impurity in faith.

6. These persons have the same defect as regards the practice of prayer, for they think that all the business of prayer consists in experiencing sensible pleasure and devotion and they strive to obtain this by great effort, wearying and fatiguing their faculties and their heads; and when they have not found this pleasure they become greatly discouraged, thinking that they have accomplished nothing. Through these efforts they lose true devotion and spirituality, which consist in perseverance, together with patience and humility, and mistrust of themselves, that they may please God alone. For this reason, when they have once failed to find pleasure in this or some other exercise, they have great disinclination and repugnance to return to it, and at times they abandon it. They are, in fact, as we have said, like children, who are not influenced by reason, and who act, not from rational motives, but from inclination. Such persons expend all their effort in seeking spiritual pleasure and consolation; they never tire, therefore, of reading books; and they begin, now one meditation, now another, in their pursuit of this pleasure which they desire to experience in the things of God. But God, very justly, wisely and lovingly, denies it to them, for otherwise this spiritual gluttony and inordinate appetite would breed innumerable evils. It is, therefore, very fitting that they should enter into the dark night, whereof we shall speak, that they may be purged from this childishness.

7. These persons who are thus inclined to such pleasures have another very great imperfection, which is that they are very weak and remiss in journeying upon the hard road of the Cross; for the soul that is given to sweetness naturally has its face set against all self-denial, which is devoid of sweetness.

8. These persons have many other imperfections which arise hence, of which in time the Lord heals them by means of temptations, aridities and other trials, all of which are part of the dark night. All these I will not treat further here, lest I become too lengthy; I will only say that spiritual temperance and sobriety lead to another and a very different temper, which is that of mortification, fear and submission in all things. It thus becomes clear that the perfection and worth of things consist not in the multitude and the pleasantness of one's actions, but in being able to deny oneself in them; this such persons must endeavour to compass, in so far as they may, until God is pleased to purify them indeed, by bringing them into the dark night, to arrive at which I am hastening on with my account of these imperfections.

CHAPTER VII

Of imperfections with respect to spiritual envy and sloth.

WITH RESPECT likewise to the other two vices, which are spiritual envy and sloth, these beginners fail not to have many imperfections. For, with respect to envy, many of them are wont to experience movements of displeasure at the spiritual good of others, which cause them a certain sensible grief at being outstripped upon this road, so that they would prefer not to hear others praised; for they become displeased at others' virtues and sometimes they cannot refrain from contradicting what is said in praise of them, depreciating it as far as they can; and their annoyance thereat grows because the same is not said of them, for they would fain be preferred in everything. All this is clean contrary to charity, which, as Saint Paul says, rejoices in goodness.[1] And, if charity has any envy, it is a holy envy, comprising grief at not having the virtues of others, yet also joy because others have them, and delight when others outstrip us in the service of God, wherein we ourselves are so remiss.

2. With respect also to spiritual sloth, beginners are apt to be irked by the things that are most spiritual, from which they flee because these things are incompatible with sensible pleasure. For, as they are so much accustomed to sweetness in spiritual things, they are wearied by things in which they find no sweetness. If once they failed to find in prayer the satisfaction which their taste required (and after all it is well that God should take it from them to prove them), they would prefer not to return to it: sometimes they leave it; at other times they continue it unwillingly. And thus because of this sloth they abandon the way of perfection (which is the way of the negation of their will and pleasure for God's sake) for the pleasure and sweetness of their own will, which they aim at satisfying in this way rather than the will of God.

3. And many of these would have God will that which they themselves will, and are fretful at having to will that which He wills, and find it repugnant to accommodate their will to that of God. Hence it happens to them that oftentimes they think that that wherein they find not their own will and pleasure is not the will of God; and that, on the other hand, when they themselves find satisfaction, God is satisfied. Thus they measure God by themselves and not themselves by God, acting quite contrarily to that which He Himself taught in the Gospel, saying: That he who should lose his will for His sake, the

---

[1] 1 Corinthians xiii, 6. The Saint here cites the sense, not the letter, of the epistle.

same should gain it; and he who should desire to gain it, the same should lose it.[2]

4. These persons likewise find it irksome when they are commanded to do that wherein they take no pleasure. Because they aim at spiritual sweetness and consolation, they are too weak to have the fortitude and bear the trials of perfection. They resemble those who are softly nurtured and who run fretfully away from everything that is hard, and take offense at the Cross, wherein consist the delights of the spirit. The more spiritual a thing is, the more irksome they find it, for, as they seek to go about spiritual matters with complete freedom and according to the inclination of their will, it causes them great sorrow and repugnance to enter upon the narrow way, which, says Christ, is the way of life.[3]

5. Let it suffice here to have described these imperfections, among the many to be found in the lives of those that are in this first state of beginners, so that it may be seen how greatly they need God to set them in the state of proficients. This He does by bringing them into the dark night whereof we now speak; wherein He weans them from the breasts of these sweetnesses and pleasures, gives them pure aridities and inward darkness, takes from them all these irrelevances and puerilities, and by very different means causes them to win the virtues. For, however assiduously the beginner practices the mortification in himself of all these actions and passions of his, he can never completely succeed—very far from it—until God shall work it in him passively by means of the purgation of the said night. Of this I would fain speak in some way that may be profitable; may God, then, be pleased to give me His Divine light, because this is very needful in a night that is so dark and a matter that is so difficult to describe and to expound.

The line, then, is:

In a dark night.

CHAPTER VIII

Wherein is expounded the first line of the first stanza, and a beginning is made of the explanation of this dark night.

THIS NIGHT which, as we say, is contemplation, produces in spiritual persons two kinds of darkness or purgation, corresponding to the two parts of man's nature—namely, the sensual and the spiritual. And thus

---

[2] St. Matthew xvi, 25.
[3] St. Matthew xii, 14.

the one night or purgation will be sensual, wherein the soul is purged according to sense, which is subdued to the spirit; and the other is a night or purgation which is spiritual, wherein the soul is purged and stripped according to the spirit, and subdued and made ready for the union of love with God. The night of sense is common and comes to many: these are the beginners; and of this night we shall speak first. The night of the spirit is the portion of very few, and these are they that are already practiced and proficient, of whom we shall treat hereafter.

2. The first purgation or night is bitter and terrible to sense, as we shall now show. The second bears no comparison with it, for it is horrible and awful to the spirit, as we shall show presently. Since the night of sense is first in order and comes first, we shall first of all say something about it briefly, since more is written of it, as of a thing that is more common; and we shall pass on to treat more fully of the spiritual night, since very little has been said of this, either in speech or in writing, and very little is known of it, even by experience.

3. Since, then, the conduct of these beginners upon the way of God is ignoble, and has much to do with their love of self and their own inclinations, as has been explained above, God desires to lead them farther. He seeks to bring them out of that ignoble kind of love to a higher degree of love for Him, to free them from the ignoble exercises of sense and meditation (wherewith, as we have said, they go seeking God so unworthily and in so many ways that are unbefitting), and to lead them to a kind of spiritual exercise wherein they can commune with Him more abundantly and are freed more completely from imperfections. For they have now had practice for some time in the way of virtue and have persevered in meditation and prayer, whereby, through the sweetness and pleasure that they have found therein, they have lost their love of the things of the world and have gained some degree of spiritual strength in God; this has enabled them to some extent to refrain from creature desires, so that for God's sake they are now able to suffer a light burden and a little aridity without turning back to a time which they found more pleasant. When they are going about these spiritual exercises with the greatest delight and pleasure, and when they believe that the sun of Divine favor is shining most brightly upon them, God turns all this light of theirs into darkness, and shuts against them the door and the source of the sweet spiritual water which they were tasting in God whensoever and for as long as they desired. (For, as they were weak and tender, there was no door closed to them, as Saint John says in the Apocalypse, iii, 8). And thus He leaves them so completely in the dark that they know not whither to go with their sensible imagination and meditation; for they cannot advance a step in meditation, as they were wont to do aforetime, their inward senses being

submerged in this night, and left with such dryness that not only do they experience no pleasure and consolation in the spiritual things and good exercises wherein they were wont to find their delights and pleasures, but instead, on the contrary, they find insipidity and bitterness in the said things. For, as I have said, God now sees that they have grown a little, and are becoming strong enough to lay aside their swaddling clothes and be taken from the gentle breast; so He sets them down from His arms and teaches them to walk on their own feet; which they feel to be very strange, for everything seems to be going wrong with them.

4. To recollected persons this commonly happens sooner after their beginnings than to others, inasmuch as they are freer from occasions of backsliding, and their desires turn more quickly from the things of the world, which is necessary if they are to begin to enter this blessed night of sense. Ordinarily no great time passes after their beginnings before they begin to enter this night of sense; and the great majority of them do in fact enter it, for they will generally be seen to fall into these aridities.

5. With regard to this way of purgation of the senses, since it is so common, we might here adduce a great number of quotations from Divine Scripture, where many passages relating to it are continually found, particularly in the Psalms and the Prophets. However, I do not wish to spend time upon these, for he who knows not how to look for them there will find the common experience of this purgation to be sufficient.

CHAPTER IX

Of the signs by which it will be known that the spiritual person is walking along the way of this night and purgation of sense.

BUT SINCE these aridities might frequently proceed, not from the night and purgation of the sensual desires aforementioned, but from sins and imperfections, or from weakness and lukewarmness, or from some bad humor or indisposition of the body, I shall here set down certain signs by which it may be known if such aridity proceeds from the aforementioned purgation, or if it arises from any of the aforementioned sins. For the making of this distinction I find that there are three principal signs.

2. The first is whether, when a soul finds no pleasure or consolation in the things of God, it also fails to find it in any thing created; for, as God sets the soul in this dark night to the end that He may quench and purge its sensual desire, He allows it not to find attraction or sweetness

in anything whatsoever. In such a case it may be considered very probable that this aridity and insipidity proceed not from recently committed sins or imperfections. For, if this were so, the soul would feel in its nature some inclination or desire to taste other things than those of God; since, whenever the desire is allowed indulgence in any imperfection, it immediately feels inclined thereto, whether little or much, in proportion to the pleasure and the love that it has put into it. Since, however, this lack of enjoyment in things above or below might proceed from some indisposition or melancholy humor, which oftentimes makes it impossible for the soul to take pleasure in anything, it becomes necessary to apply the second sign and condition.

3. The second sign whereby a man may believe himself to be experiencing the said purgation is that the memory is ordinarily centred upon God, with painful care and solicitude, thinking that it is not serving God, but is backsliding, because it finds itself without sweetness in the things of God. And in such a case it is evident that this lack of sweetness and this aridity come not from weakness and lukewarmness; for it is the nature of lukewarmness not to care greatly or to have any inward solicitude for the things of God. There is thus a great difference between aridity and lukewarmness, for lukewarmness consists in great weakness and remissness in the will and in the spirit, without solicitude as to serving God; whereas purgative aridity is ordinarily accompanied by solicitude, with care and grief, as I say, because the soul is not serving God. And, although this may sometimes be increased by melancholy or some other humor (as it frequently is), it fails not for that reason to produce a purgative effect upon the desire, since the desire is deprived of all pleasure, and has its care centered upon God alone. For, when mere humor is the cause, it spends itself in displeasure and ruin of the physical nature, and there are none of those desires to serve God which belong to purgative aridity. When the cause is aridity, it is true that the sensual part of the soul has fallen low, and is weak and feeble in its actions, by reason of the little pleasure which it finds in them; but the spirit, on the other hand, is ready and strong.

4. For the cause of this aridity is that God transfers to the spirit the good things and the strength of the senses, which, since the soul's natural strength and senses are incapable of using them, remain barren, dry and empty. For the sensual part of a man has no capacity for that which is pure spirit, and thus, when it is the spirit that receives the pleasure, the flesh is left without savour and is too weak to perform any action. But the spirit, which all the time is being fed, goes forward in strength, and with more alertness and solicitude than before, in its anxiety not to fail God; and if it is not immediately conscious of spiritual sweetness and delight, but only of aridity and lack of sweetness, the reason for this

is the strangeness of the exchange; for its palate has been accustomed to those other sensual pleasures upon which its eyes are still fixed, and, since the spiritual palate is not made ready or purged for such subtle pleasure, until it finds itself becoming prepared for it by means of this arid and dark night, it cannot experience spiritual pleasure and good, but only aridity and lack of sweetness, since it misses the pleasure which aforetime it enjoyed so readily.

5. These souls whom God is beginning to lead through these solitary places of the wilderness are like to the children of Israel, to whom in the wilderness God began to give food from Heaven, containing within itself all sweetness, and, as is there said, it turned to the savour which each one of them desired. But withal the children of Israel felt the lack of the pleasures and delights of the flesh and the onions which they had eaten aforetime in Egypt, the more so because their palate was accustomed to these and took delight in them, rather than in the delicate sweetness of the angelic manna; and they wept and sighed for the fleshpots even in the midst of the food of Heaven.[1] To such depths does the vileness of our desires descend that it makes us to long for our own wretched food and to be nauseated by the indescribable blessings of Heaven.

6. But, as I say, when these aridities proceed from the way of the purgation of sensual desire, although at first the spirit feels no sweetness, for the reasons that we have just given, it feels that it is deriving strength and energy to act from the substance which this inward food gives it, the which food is the beginning of a contemplation that is dark and arid to the senses; which contemplation is secret and hidden from the very person that experiences it; and ordinarily, together with the aridity and emptiness which it causes in the senses, it gives the soul an inclination and desire to be alone and in quietness, without being able to think of any particular thing or having the desire to do so. If those souls to whom this comes to pass knew how to be quiet at this time, and troubled not about performing any kind of action, whether inward or outward, neither had any anxiety about doing anything, then they would delicately experience this inward refreshment in that ease and freedom from care. So delicate is this refreshment that ordinarily, if a man have desire or care to experience it, he experiences it not; for, as I say, it does its work when the soul is most at ease and freest from care; it is like the air which, if one would close one's hand upon it, escapes.

7. In this sense we may understand that which the Spouse said to the Bride in the Songs, namely: "Withdraw thine eyes from me, for they make

---

[1] Numbers xi, 5–6.

me to soar aloft."[2] For in such a way does God bring the soul into this state, and by so different a path does He lead it that, if it desires to work with its faculties, it hinders the work which God is doing in it rather than aids it; whereas aforetime it was quite the contrary. The reason is that, in this state of contemplation, which the soul enters when it forsakes meditation for the state of the proficient, it is God Who is now working in the soul; He binds its interior faculties, and allows it not to cling to the understanding, nor to have delight in the will, nor to reason with the memory. For anything that the soul can do of its own accord at this time serves only, as we have said, to hinder inward peace and the work which God is accomplishing in the spirit by means of that aridity of sense. And this peace, being spiritual and delicate, performs a work which is quiet and delicate, solitary, productive of peace and satisfaction and far removed from all those earlier pleasures, which were very palpable and sensual. This is the peace which, says David, God speaks in the soul to the end that He may make it spiritual.[3] And this leads us to the third point.

8. The third sign whereby this purgation of sense may be recognized is that the soul can no longer meditate or reflect in the imaginative sphere of sense as it was wont, however much it may of itself endeavour to do so. For God now begins to communicate Himself to it, no longer through sense, as He did aforetime, by means of reflections which joined and sundered its knowledge, but by pure spirit, into which consecutive reflections enter not; but He communicates Himself to it by an act of simple contemplation, to which neither the exterior nor the interior senses of the lower part of the soul can attain. From this time forward, therefore, imagination and fancy can find no support in any meditation, and can gain no foothold by means thereof.

9. With regard to this third sign, it is to be understood that this embarrassment and dissatisfaction of the faculties proceed not from indisposition, for, when this is the case, and the indisposition, which never lasts for long, comes to an end, the soul is able once again, by taking some trouble about the matter, to do what it did before, and the faculties find their wonted support. But in the purgation of the desire this is not so: when once the soul begins to enter therein, its inability to reflect with the faculties grows ever greater. For, although it is true that at first, and with some persons, the process is not as continuous as this, so that occasionally they fail to abandon their pleasures and reflections of sense (for perchance by reason of their weakness it was not fitting to wean them

---

[2] Canticles vi, 5.
[3] Psalm lxxxv, 8.

from these immediately), yet this inability grows within them more and more and brings the workings of sense to an end, if indeed they are to make progress, for those who walk not in the way of contemplation act very differently. For this night of aridities is not usually continuous in their senses. At times they have these aridities; at others they have them not. At times they cannot meditate; at others they can. For God sets them in this night only to prove them and to humble them, and to reform their desires, so that they go not nurturing in themselves a sinful gluttony in spiritual things. He sets them not there in order to lead them in the way of the spirit, which is this contemplation; for not all those who walk of set purpose in the way of the spirit are brought by God to contemplation, nor even the half of them—why, He best knows. And this is why He never completely weans the senses of such persons from the breasts of meditations and reflections, but only for short periods and at certain seasons, as we have said.

CHAPTER X

Of the way in which these souls are to conduct themselves in this dark night.

DURING THE time, then, of the aridities of this night of sense (wherein God effects the change of which we have spoken above, drawing forth the soul from the life of sense into that of the spirit—that is, from meditation to contemplation—wherein it no longer has any power to work or to reason with its faculties concerning the things of God, as has been said), spiritual persons suffer great trials, by reason not so much of the aridities which they suffer, as of the fear which they have of being lost on the road, thinking that all spiritual blessing is over for them and that God has abandoned them since they find no help or pleasure in good things. Then they grow weary, and endeavour (as they have been accustomed to do) to concentrate their faculties with some degree of pleasure upon some object of meditation, thinking that, when they are not doing this and yet are conscious of making an effort, they are doing nothing. This effort they make not without great inward repugnance and unwillingness on the part of their soul, which was taking pleasure in being in that quietness and ease, instead of working with its faculties. So they have abandoned the one pursuit, yet draw no profit from the other; for, by seeking what is prompted by their own spirit, they lose the spirit of tranquillity and peace which they had before. And thus they are like to one who abandons what he has done in order to do it over again, or to one who leaves a city only to re-enter it, or to one who is hunting and lets his prey go in order to hunt it once more. This is useless here, for the soul will gain nothing further by conducting itself in this way, as has been said.

2. These souls turn back at such a time if there is none who understands them; they abandon the road or lose courage; or, at the least, they are hindered from going farther by the great trouble which they take in advancing along the road of meditation and reasoning. Thus they fatigue and overwork their nature, imagining that they are failing through negligence or sin. But this trouble that they are taking is quite useless, for God is now leading them by another road, which is that of contemplation, and is very different from the first; for the one is of meditation and reasoning, and the other belongs neither to imagination nor yet to reasoning.

3. It is well for those who find themselves in this condition to take comfort, to persevere in patience and to be in no wise afflicted. Let them trust in God, Who abandons not those that seek Him with a simple and right heart, and will not fail to give them what is needful for the road, until He bring them into the clear and pure light of love. This last He will give them by means of that other dark night, that of the spirit, if they merit His bringing them thereto.

4. The way in which they are to conduct themselves in this night of sense is to devote themselves not at all to reasoning and meditation, since this is not the time for it, but to allow the soul to remain in peace and quietness, although it may seem clear to them that they are doing nothing and are wasting their time, and although it may appear to them that it is because of their weakness that they have no desire in that state to think of anything. The truth is that they will be doing quite sufficient if they have patience and persevere in prayer without making any effort. What they must do is merely to leave the soul free and disencumbered and at rest from all knowledge and thought, troubling not themselves, in that state, about what they shall think or meditate upon, but contenting themselves with merely a peaceful and loving attentiveness toward God, and in being without anxiety, without the ability and without desire to have experience of Him or to perceive Him. For all these yearnings disquiet and distract the soul from the peaceful quiet and sweet ease of contemplation which is here granted to it.

5. And although further scruples may come to them—that they are wasting their time, and that it would be well for them to do something else, because they can neither do nor think anything in prayer—let them suffer these scruples and remain in peace, as there is no question save of their being at ease and having freedom of spirit. For if such a

soul should desire to make any effort of its own with its interior faculties, this means that it will hinder and lose the blessings which, by means of that peace and ease of the soul, God is instilling into it and impressing upon it. It is just as if some painter were painting or dyeing a face; if the sitter were to move because he desired to do something, he would prevent the painter from accomplishing anything and would disturb him in what he was doing. And thus, when the soul desires to remain in inward ease and peace, any operation and affection or attention wherein it may then seek to indulge will distract it and disquiet it and make it conscious of aridity and emptiness of sense. For the more a soul endeavours to find support in affection and knowledge, the more will it feel the lack of these, which cannot now be supplied to it upon that road.

6. Wherefore it behoves such a soul to pay no heed if the operations of its faculties become lost to it; it is rather to desire that this should happen quickly. For, by not hindering the operation of infused contemplation that God is bestowing upon it, it can receive this with more peaceful abundance, and cause its spirit to be enkindled and to burn with the love which this dark and secret contemplation brings with it and sets firmly in the soul. For contemplation is naught else than a secret, peaceful and loving infusion from God, which, if it be permitted, enkindles the soul with the spirit of love, according as the soul declares in the next lines, namely:

Kindled in love with yearnings.

CHAPTER XI

Wherein are expounded the three lines of the stanza.

THIS ENKINDLING of love is not as a rule felt at the first, because it has not begun to take hold upon the soul, by reason of the impurity of human nature, or because the soul has not understood its own state, as we have said, and has therefore given it no peaceful abiding-place within itself. Yet sometimes, nevertheless, there soon begins to make itself felt a certain yearning toward God; and the more this increases, the more is the soul affectioned and enkindled in love toward God, without knowing or understanding how and whence this love and affection come to it, but from time to time seeing this flame and this enkindling grow so greatly within it that it desires God with yearning of love; even as David, when he was in this dark night, said of himself in these words,[1] namely: "Because my heart was enkindled (that is to say, in love of contemplation), my reins also were changed": that is, my desires for sensual affections were changed, namely from the way of sense to the way of the spirit, which is the aridity and cessation from all these things whereof we are speaking. And I, he says, was dissolved in nothing and annihilated, and I knew not; for, as we have said, without knowing the way whereby it goes, the soul finds itself annihilated with respect to all things above and below which were accustomed to please it; and it finds itself enamoured, without knowing how. And because at times the enkindling of love in the spirit grows greater, the yearnings for God become so great in the soul that the very bones seem to be dried up by this thirst, and the natural powers to be fading away, and their warmth and strength to be perishing through the intensity of the thirst of love, for the soul feels that this thirst of love is a living thirst. This thirst David had and felt, when he said: "My soul thirsted for the living God."[2] Which is as much as to say: A living thirst was that of my soul. Of this thirst, since it is living, we may say that it kills. But it is to be noted that the vehemence of this thirst is not continuous, but occasional, although as a rule the soul is accustomed to feel it to a certain degree.

2. But it must be noted that, as I began to say just now, this love is not as a rule felt at first, but only the dryness and emptiness are felt whereof we are speaking. Then in place of this love which afterwards becomes gradually enkindled, what the soul experiences in the midst of these aridities and emptinesses of the faculties is an habitual care and solicitude with respect to God, together with grief and fear that it is not serving Him. But it is a sacrifice which is not a little pleasing to God that the soul should go about afflicted and solicitous for His love. This solicitude and care leads the soul into that secret contemplation, until, the senses (that is, the sensual part) having in course of time been in some degree purged of the natural affections and powers by means of the aridities which it causes within them, this Divine love begins to be enkindled in the spirit. Meanwhile, however, like one who has begun a cure, the soul knows only suffering in this dark and arid purgation of the desire; by this means it becomes healed of many imperfections, and exercises itself in many virtues in order to make itself meet for the said love, as we shall now say with respect to the line following:

Oh, happy chance!

---

[1] Psalm lxxiii, 21.
[2] Psalm xlii, 2.

3. When God leads the soul into this night of sense in order to purge the sense of its lower part and to subdue it, unite it and bring it into conformity with the spirit, by setting it in darkness and causing it to cease from meditation (as He afterwards does in order to purify the spirit to unite it with God, as we shall afterwards say), He brings it into the night of the spirit, and (although it appears not so to it) the soul gains so many benefits that it holds it to be a happy chance to have escaped from the bonds and restrictions of the senses of its lower self, by means of this night aforesaid; and utters the present line, namely: Oh, happy chance! With respect to this, it behoves us here to note the benefits which the soul finds in this night, and because of which it considers it a happy chance to have passed through it; all of which benefits the soul includes in the next line, namely:

I went forth without being observed.

4. This going forth is understood of the subjection to its sensual part which the soul suffered when it sought God through operations so weak, so limited and so defective as are those of this lower part; for at every step it stumbled into numerous imperfections and ignorances, as we have noted above in writing of the seven capital sins. From all these it is freed when this night quenches within it all pleasures, whether from above or from below, and makes all meditation darkness to it, and grants it other innumerable blessings in the acquirement of the virtues, as we shall now show. For it will be a matter of great pleasure and great consolation, to one that journeys on this road, to see how that which seems to the soul so severe and adverse, and so contrary to spiritual pleasure, works in it so many blessings. These, as we say, are gained when the soul goes forth, as regards its affection and operation, by means of this night, from all created things, and when it journeys to eternal things, which is great happiness and good fortune: first, because of the great blessing which is in the quenching of the desire and affection with respect to all things; secondly, because they are very few that endure and persevere in entering by this strait gate and by the narrow way which leads to life, as says Our Saviour.[3] The strait gate is this night of sense, and the soul detaches itself from sense and strips itself thereof that it may enter by this gate, and establishes itself in faith, which is a stranger to all sense, so that afterwards it may journey by the narrow way, which is the other night—that of the spirit—and this the soul afterwards enters in order to journey to God in pure faith, which is the

---

[3] St. Matthew vii, 14.

means whereby the soul is united to God. By this road, since it is so narrow, dark and terrible (though there is no comparison between this night of sense and that other, in its darkness and trials, as we shall say later), they are far fewer that journey, but its benefits are far greater without comparison than those of this present night. Of these benefits we shall now begin to say something, with such brevity as is possible, in order that we may pass to the other night.

CHAPTER XII

Of the benefits which this night causes in the soul.

THIS NIGHT and purgation of the desire, a happy one for the soul, works in it so many blessings and benefits (although to the soul, as we have said, it rather seems that blessings are being taken away from it) that, even as Abraham made a great feast when he weaned his son Isaac,[1] even so is there joy in Heaven because God is now taking this soul from its swaddling clothes, setting it down from His arms, making it to walk upon its feet, and likewise taking from it the milk of the breast and the soft and sweet food proper to children, and making it to eat bread with crust, and to begin to enjoy the food of robust persons. This food, in these aridities and this darkness of sense, is now given to the spirit, which is dry and emptied of all the sweetness of sense. And this food is the infused contemplation whereof we have spoken.

2. This is the first and principal benefit caused by this arid and dark night of contemplation: the knowledge of oneself and of one's misery. For, besides the fact that all the favors which God grants to the soul are habitually granted to them enwrapped in this knowledge, these aridities and this emptiness of the faculties, compared with the abundance which the soul experienced aforetime and the difficulty which it finds in good works, make it recognize its own lowliness and misery, which in the time of its prosperity it was unable to see. Of this there is a good illustration in the Book of Exodus, where God, wishing to humble the children of Israel and desiring that they should know themselves, commanded them to take away and strip off the festal garments and adornments wherewith they were accustomed to adorn themselves in the Wilderness, saying: "Now from henceforth strip yourselves of festal ornaments and put on

---

[1] Genesis xxi, 8.

everyday working dress, that ye may know what treatment ye deserve."[2]
This is as though He had said: Inasmuch as the attire that ye wear,
being proper to festival and rejoicing, causes you to feel less humble
concerning yourselves than ye should, put off from you this attire, in
order that henceforth, seeing yourselves clothed with vileness, ye may
know that ye merit no more, and may know who ye are. Wherefore the
soul knows the truth that it knew not at first, concerning its own misery; for, at the time when it was clad as for a festival and found in God
much pleasure, consolation and support, it was somewhat more satisfied and contented, since it thought itself to some extent to be serving
God. It is true that such souls may not have this idea explicitly in their
minds; but some suggestion of it at least is implanted in them by the
satisfaction which they find in their pleasant experiences. But, now that
the soul has put on its other and working attire—that of aridity and
abandonment—and now that its first lights have turned into darkness,
it possesses these lights more truly in this virtue of self-knowledge,
which is so excellent and so necessary, considering itself now as nothing and experiencing no satisfaction in itself; for it sees that it does
nothing of itself neither can do anything. And the smallness of this self-
satisfaction, together with the soul's affliction at not serving God, is
considered and esteemed by God as greater than all the consolations
which the soul formerly experienced and the works which it wrought,
however great they were, inasmuch as they were the occasion of many
imperfections and ignorances. And from this attire of aridity proceed,
as from their fount and source of self-knowledge, not only the things
which we have described already, but also the benefits which we shall
now describe and many more which will have to be omitted.

3. In the first place, the soul learns to commune with God with more
respect and more courtesy, such as a soul must ever observe in converse
with the Most High. These it knew not in its prosperous times of comfort and consolation, for that comforting favor which it experienced
made its craving for God somewhat bolder than was fitting, and dis-
courteous and ill-considered. Even so did it happen to Moses, when he
perceived that God was speaking to him; blinded by that pleasure and
desire, without further consideration, he would have made bold to go
to Him if God had not commanded him to stay and put off his shoes.
By this incident we are shown the respect and discretion in detachment
of desire wherewith a man is to commune with God. When Moses had
obeyed in this matter, he became so discreet and so attentive that the

---

[2] Exodus xxxiii, 5.

Scripture says that not only did he not make bold to draw near to God, but that he dared not even look at Him. For, having taken off the shoes of his desires and pleasures, he became very conscious of his wretchedness in the sight of God, as befitted one about to hear the word of God. Even so likewise the preparation which God granted to Job in order that he might speak with Him consisted not in those delights and glories which Job himself reports that he was wont to have in his God, but in leaving him naked upon a dung-hill,[3] abandoned and even persecuted by his friends, filled with anguish and bitterness, and the earth covered with worms. And then the Most High God, He that lifts up the poor man from the dung-hill, was pleased to come down and speak with him there face to face, revealing to him the depths and heights of His wisdom, in a way that He had never done in the time of his prosperity.

4. And here we must note another excellent benefit which there is in this night and aridity of the desire of sense, since we have had occasion to speak of it. It is that, in this dark night of the desire (to the end that the words of the Prophet may be fulfilled, namely: "Thy light shall shine in the darkness"[4]), God will enlighten the soul, giving it knowledge, not only of its lowliness and wretchedness, as we have said, but likewise of the greatness and excellence of God. For, as well as quenching the desires and pleasures and attachments of sense, He cleanses and frees the understanding that it may understand the truth; for pleasure of sense and desire, even though it be for spiritual things, darkens and obstructs the spirit, and furthermore that straitness and aridity of sense enlightens and quickens the understanding, as says Isaias.[5] Vexation makes us to understand how the soul that is empty and disencumbered, as is necessary for His Divine influence, is instructed supernaturally by God in His Divine wisdom, through this dark and arid night of contemplation, as we have said; and this instruction God gave not in those first sweetnesses and joys.

5. This is very well explained by the same prophet Isaias, where he says: "Whom shall God teach His knowledge, and whom shall He make to understand the hearing?" To those, He says, that are weaned from the milk and drawn away from the breasts.[6] Here it is shown that the first milk of spiritual sweetness is no preparation for this Divine influence, neither is there preparation in attachment to the breast of delectable meditations, belonging to the faculties of sense, which gave

---

[3] [Job ii, 7–8.]
[4] Isaias lviii, 10.
[5] Isaias xxviii, 19. [The author omits the actual text.]
[6] Isaias xxviii, 9.

the soul pleasure; such preparation consists rather in the lack of the one and withdrawal from the other. Inasmuch as, in order to listen to God, the soul needs to stand upright and to be detached, with regard to affection and sense, even as the Prophet says concerning himself, in these words: I will stand upon my watch (this is that detachment of desire) and I will make firm my step (that is, I will not meditate with sense), in order to contemplate (that is, in order to understand that which may come to me from God).[7] So we have now arrived at this, that from this arid night there first of all comes self-knowledge, whence, as from a foundation, rises this other knowledge of God. For which cause Saint Augustine said to God: "Let me know myself, Lord, and I shall know Thee."[8] For, as the philosophers say, one extreme can be well known by another.

6. And in order to prove more completely how efficacious is this night of sense, with its aridity and its desolation, in bringing the soul that light which, as we say, it receives there from God, we shall quote that passage of David, wherein he clearly describes the great power which is in this night for bringing the soul this lofty knowledge of God. He says, then, thus: "In the desert land, waterless, dry and pathless, I appeared before Thee, that I might see Thy virtue and Thy glory."[9] It is a wondrous thing that David should say here that the means and the preparation for his knowledge of the glory of God were not the spiritual delights and the many pleasures which he had experienced, but the aridities and detachments of his sensual nature, which is here to be understood by the dry and desert land. No less wondrous is it that he should describe as the road to his perception and vision of the virtue of God, not the Divine meditations and conceptions of which he had often made use, but his being unable to form any conception of God or to walk by meditation produced by imaginary consideration, which is here to be understood by the pathless land. So that the means to a knowledge of God and of oneself is this dark night with its aridities and voids, although it leads not to a knowledge of Him of the same plenitude and abundance that comes from the other night of the spirit, since this is only, as it were, the beginning of that other.

7. Likewise, from the aridities and voids of this night of the desire, the soul draws spiritual humility, which is the contrary virtue to the first capital sin, which, as we said, is spiritual pride. Through this humility, which is acquired by the said knowledge of self, the soul is purged from

---

[7] Habacuc ii, I.
[8] St. Augustine: *Soliloq.*, Cap. ii.
[9] Psalm lxiii, 1–2.

all those imperfections whereinto it fell with respect to that sin of pride, in the time of its prosperity. For it sees itself so dry and miserable that the idea never even occurs to it that it is making better progress than others, or outstripping them, as it believed itself to be doing before. On the contrary, it recognizes that others are making better progress than itself.

8. And hence arises the love of its neighbors, for it esteems them, and judges them not as it was wont to do aforetime, when it saw that itself had great fervour and others not so. It is aware only of its own wretchedness, which it keeps before its eyes to such an extent that it never forgets it, nor takes occasion to set its eyes on anyone else. This was described wonderfully by David, when he was in this night, in these words: "I was dumb and was humbled and kept silence from good things and my sorrow was renewed."[10] This he says because it seemed to him that the good that was in his soul had so completely departed that not only did he neither speak nor find any language concerning it, but with respect to the good of others he was likewise dumb because of his grief at the knowledge of his misery.

9. In this condition, again, souls become submissive and obedient upon the spiritual road, for, when they see their own misery, not only do they hear what is taught them, but they even desire that anyone soever may set them on the way and tell them what they ought to do. The affective presumption which they sometimes had in their prosperity is taken from them; and finally, there are swept away from them on this road all the other imperfections which we noted above with respect to this first sin, which is spiritual pride.

CHAPTER XIII

Of other benefits which this night of sense causes in the soul.

WITH RESPECT to the soul's imperfections of spiritual avarice, because of which it coveted this and that spiritual thing and found no satisfaction in this and that exercise by reason of its covetousness for the desire and pleasure which it found therein, this arid and dark night has now greatly reformed it. For, as it finds not the pleasure and sweetness which it was wont to find, but rather finds affliction and lack of sweetness, it has such moderate recourse to them that it might possibly now lose, through defective use, what aforetime it lost through excess; although as a rule

---

[10] Psalm xxxix, 2.

God gives to those whom He leads into this night humility and readiness, albeit with lack of sweetness, so that what is commanded them they may do for God's sake alone; and thus they no longer seek profit in many things because they find no pleasure in them.

2. With respect to spiritual luxury, it is likewise clearly seen that, through this aridity and lack of sensible sweetness which the soul finds in spiritual things, it is freed from those impurities which we there noted; for we said that, as a rule, they proceeded from the pleasure which overflowed from spirit into sense.

3. But with regard to the imperfections from which the soul frees itself in this dark night with respect to the fourth sin, which is spiritual gluttony, they may be found above, though they have not all been described there, because they are innumerable; and thus I will not detail them here, for I would fain make an end of this night in order to pass to the next, concerning which we shall have to pronounce grave words and instructions. Let it suffice for the understanding of the innumerable benefits which, over and above those mentioned, the soul gains in this night with respect to this sin of spiritual gluttony, to say that it frees itself from all those imperfections which have there been described, and from many other and greater evils, and vile abominations which are not written above, into which fell many of whom we have had experience, because they had not reformed their desire as concerning this inordinate love of spiritual sweetness. For in this arid and dark night wherein He sets the soul, God has restrained its concupiscence and curbed its desire so that the soul cannot feed upon any pleasure or sweetness of sense, whether from above or from below; and this He continues to do after such manner that the soul is subjected, reformed and repressed with respect to concupiscence and desire. It loses the strength of its passions and concupiscence and it becomes sterile, because it no longer consults its likings. Just as, when none is accustomed to take milk from the breast, the courses of the milk are dried up, so the desires of the soul are dried up. And besides these things there follow admirable benefits from this spiritual sobriety, for, when desire and concupiscence are quenched, the soul lives in spiritual tranquillity and peace; for, where desire and concupiscence reign not, there is no disturbance, but peace and consolation of God.

4. From this there arises another and a second benefit, which is that the soul habitually has remembrance of God, with fear and dread of backsliding upon the spiritual road, as has been said. This is a great benefit, and not one of the least that results from this aridity and purgation of the desire, for the soul is purified and cleansed of the imperfections that were clinging to it because of the desires and affections, which of their own accord deaden and darken the soul.

5. There is another very great benefit for the soul in this night, which is that it practices several virtues together, as, for example, patience and longsuffering, which are often called upon in these times of emptiness and aridity, when the soul endures and perseveres in its spiritual exercises without consolation and without pleasure. It practices the charity of God, since it is not now moved by the pleasure of attraction and sweetness which it finds in its work, but only by God. It likewise practices here the virtue of fortitude, because, in these difficulties and insipidities which it finds in its work, it brings strength out of weakness and thus becomes strong. All the virtues, in short—the theological and also the cardinal and moral—both in body and in spirit, are practiced by the soul in these times of aridity.

6. And that in this night the soul obtains these four benefits which we have here described (namely, delight of peace, habitual remembrance and thought of God, cleanness and purity of soul and the practice of the virtues which we have just described), David tells us, having experienced it himself when he was in this night, in these words: "My soul refused consolations, I had remembrance of God, I found consolation and was exercised and my spirit failed."[1] And he then says: "And I meditated by night with my heart and was exercised, and I swept and purified my spirit"—that is to say, from all the affections.[2]

7. With respect to the imperfections of the other three spiritual sins which we have described above, which are wrath, envy and sloth, the soul is purged hereof likewise in this aridity of the desire and acquires the virtues opposed to them; for, softened and humbled by these aridities and hardships and other temptations and trials wherein God exercises it during this night, it becomes meek with respect to God, and to itself, and likewise with respect to its neighbour. So that it is no longer disturbed and angry with itself because of its own faults, nor with its neighbour because of his, neither is it displeased with God, nor does it utter unseemly complaints because He does not quickly make it holy.

8. Then, as to envy, the soul has charity toward others in this respect also; for, if it has any envy, this is no longer a vice as it was before, when it was grieved because others were preferred to it and given greater advantage. Its grief now comes from seeing how great is its own misery, and its envy (if it has any) is a virtuous envy, since it desires to imitate others, which is great virtue.

9. Neither are the sloth and the irksomeness which it now experiences concerning spiritual things vicious as they were before. For in the

---

[1] Psalm lxxvii, 3–4.
[2] Psalm lxxvii, 6.

past these sins proceeded from the spiritual pleasures which the soul sometimes experienced and sought after when it found them not. But this new weariness proceeds not from this insufficiency of pleasure, because God has taken from the soul pleasure in all things in this purgation of the desire.

10. Besides these benefits which have been mentioned, the soul attains innumerable others by means of this arid contemplation. For often, in the midst of these times of aridity and hardship, God communicates to the soul, when it is least expecting it, the purest spiritual sweetness and love, together with a spiritual knowledge which is sometimes very delicate, each manifestation of which is of greater benefit and worth than those which the soul enjoyed aforetime; although in its beginnings the soul thinks that this is not so, for the spiritual influence now granted to it is very delicate and cannot be perceived by sense.

11. Finally, inasmuch as the soul is now purged from the affections and desires of sense, it obtains liberty of spirit, whereby in ever greater degree it gains the twelve fruits of the Holy Spirit. Here, too, it is wondrously delivered from the hands of its three enemies—devil, world and flesh; for, its pleasure and delight of sense being quenched with respect to all things, neither the devil nor the world nor sensuality has any arms or any strength wherewith to make war upon the spirit.

12. These times of aridity, then, cause the soul to journey in all purity in the love of God, since it is no longer influenced in its actions by the pleasure and sweetness of the actions themselves, as perchance it was when it experienced sweetness, but only by a desire to please God. It becomes neither presumptuous nor self-satisfied, as perchance it was wont to become in the time of its prosperity, but fearful and timid with regard to itself, finding in itself no satisfaction whatsoever; and herein consists that holy fear which preserves and increases the virtues. This aridity, too, quenches natural energy and concupiscence, as has also been said. Save for the pleasure, indeed, which at certain times God Himself infuses into it, it is a wonder if it finds pleasure and consolation of sense, through its own diligence, in any spiritual exercise or action, as has already been said.

13. There grows within souls that experience this arid night concern for God and yearnings to serve Him, for in proportion as the breasts of sensuality, wherewith it sustained and nourished the desires that it pursued, are drying up, there remains nothing in that aridity and detachment save the yearning to serve God, which is a thing very pleasing to God. For, as David says, an afflicted spirit is a sacrifice to God.[3]

---

[3] Psalm li, 17.

14. When the soul, then, knows that, in this arid purgation through which it has passed, it has derived and attained so many and such precious benefits as those which have here been described, it tarries not in crying, as in the stanza of which we are expounding the lines, "Oh, happy chance!—I went forth without being observed." That is, "I went forth" from the bonds and subjection of the desires of sense and the affections, "without being observed"—that is to say, without the three enemies aforementioned being able to keep me from it. These enemies, as we have said, bind the soul as with bonds, in its desires and pleasures, and prevent it from going forth from itself to the liberty of the love of God; and without these desires and pleasures they cannot give battle to the soul, as has been said.

15. When, therefore, the four passions of the soul—which are joy, grief, hope and fear—are calmed through continual mortification; when the natural desires have been lulled to sleep, in the sensual nature of the soul, by means of habitual times of aridity; and when the harmony of the senses and the interior faculties causes a suspension of labor and a cessation from the work of meditation, as we have said (which is the dwelling and the household of the lower part of the soul), these enemies cannot obstruct this spiritual liberty, and the house remains at rest and quiet, as says the following line:

My house being now at rest.

CHAPTER XIV

Expounds this last line of the first stanza.

WHEN THIS house of sensuality was now at rest—that is, was mortified—its passions being quenched and its desires put to rest and lulled to sleep by means of this blessed night of the purgation of sense, the soul went forth, to set out upon the road and way of the spirit, which is that of progressives and proficients, and which, by another name, is called the way of illumination or of infused contemplation, wherein God Himself feeds and refreshes the soul, without meditation, or the soul's active help. Such, as we have said, is the night and purgation of sense in the soul. In those who have afterwards to enter the other and more formidable night of the spirit, in order to pass to the Divine union of love of God (for not all pass habitually thereto, but only the smallest number), it is wont to be accompanied by formidable trials and temptations of sense, which last for a long time, albeit longer in some than in others. For to some the angel of Satan presents himself—namely, the spirit of fornication—that he may buffet their senses with abominable and violent temptations, and trouble their spirits with vile considerations and representations which are most visible to the imagination, which things at times are a greater affliction to them than death.

2. At other times in this night there is added to these things the spirit of blasphemy, which roams abroad, setting in the path of all the conceptions and thoughts of the soul intolerable blasphemies. These it sometimes suggests to the imagination with such violence that the soul almost utters them, which is a grave torment to it.

3. At other times another abominable spirit, which Isaias calls *Spiritus vertiginis*,[1] is allowed to molest them, not in order that they may fall, but that it may try them. This spirit darkens their senses in such a way that it fills them with numerous scruples and perplexities, so confusing that, as they judge, they can never, by any means, be satisfied concerning them, neither can they find any help for their judgment in counsel or thought. This is one of the severest goads and horrors of this night, very closely akin to that which passes in the night of the spirit.

4. As a rule these storms and trials are sent by God in this night and purgation of sense to those whom afterwards He purposes to lead into the other night (though not all reach it), to the end that, when they have been chastened and buffeted, they may in this way continually exercise and prepare themselves, and continually accustom their senses and faculties to the union of wisdom which is to be bestowed upon them in that other night. For, if the soul be not tempted, exercised and proved with trials and temptations, it cannot quicken its sense for Wisdom. For this reason it is said in Ecclesiasticus: "He that has not been tempted, what does he know? And he that has not been proved, what are the things that he recognizes?"[2] To this truth Jeremias bears good witness, saying: "Thou didst chastise me, Lord, and I was instructed."[3] And the most proper form of this chastisement, for one who will enter into Wisdom, is that of the interior trials which we are here describing, inasmuch as it is these which most effectively purge sense of all favors and consolations to which it was affected, with natural weakness, and by which the soul is truly humiliated in preparation for the exaltation which it is to experience.

---

[1] "Spirit of giddiness" or "perverse spirit." [Isaias xix, 14.]
[2] Ecclesiasticus xxxiv, 9–10.
[3] Jeremias xxxi, 18.

5. For how long a time the soul will be held in this fasting and penance of sense, cannot be said with any certainty; for all do not experience it after one manner, neither do all encounter the same temptations. For this is meted out by the will of God, in conformity with the greater or the smaller degree of imperfection which each soul has to purge away. In conformity, likewise, with the degree of love of union to which God is pleased to raise it, He will humble it with greater or less intensity or in greater or less time. Those who have the disposition and greater strength to suffer, He purges with greater intensity and more quickly. But those who are very weak are kept for a long time in this night, and these He purges very gently and with slight temptations. Habitually, too, He gives them refreshments of sense so that they may not fall away, and only after a long time do they attain to purity of perfection in this life, some of them never attaining to it at all. Such are neither properly in the night nor properly out of it; for, although they make no progress, yet, in order that they may continue in humility and self-knowledge, God exercises them for certain periods and at certain times in those temptations and aridities; and at other times and seasons He assists them with consolations, lest they should grow faint and return to seek the consolations of the world. Other souls, which are weaker, God Himself accompanies, now appearing to them, now moving farther away, that He may exercise them in His love; for without such turnings away they would not learn to reach God.

6. But the souls which are to pass on to that happy and high estate, the union of love, are wont as a rule to remain for a long time in these aridities and temptations, however quickly God may lead them, as has been seen by experience. It is time, then, to begin to treat of the second night.

BOOK THE SECOND

Of the Dark Night of the Spirit.

CHAPTER I

Which begins to treat of the dark night of the spirit and says at what time it begins.

THE SOUL which God is about to lead onward is not led by His Majesty into this night of the spirit as soon as it goes forth from the aridities and trials of the first purgation and night of sense; rather it is wont to pass a long time, even years, after leaving the state of beginners, in exercising itself in that of proficients. In this latter state it is like to one that has come forth from a rigorous imprisonment; it goes about the things of God with much greater freedom and satisfaction of the soul, and with more abundant and inward delight than it did at the beginning before it entered the said night. For its imagination and faculties are no longer bound, as they were before, by meditation and anxiety of spirit, since it now very readily finds in its spirit the most serene and loving contemplation and spiritual sweetness without the labor of meditation; although, as the purgation of the soul is not complete (for the principal part thereof, which is that of the spirit, is wanting, without which, owing to the communication that exists between the one part and the other, since the subject is one only, the purgation of sense, however violent it may have been, is not yet complete and perfect), it is never without certain occasional necessities, aridities, darknesses and perils which are sometimes much more intense than those of the past, for they are as tokens and heralds of the coming night of the spirit, and are not of as long duration as will be the night which is to come. For, having passed through a period, or periods, or days of this night and tempest, the soul soon returns to its wonted serenity; and after this manner God purges certain souls which are not to rise to so high a degree of love as are others, bringing them at times, and for short periods, into this night of contemplation and purgation of the spirit, causing night to come upon them and then dawn, and this frequently, so that the words of David may be fulfilled, that He sends His crystal—that is, His contemplation—like morsels;[1] although these morsels of dark contemplation are never as intense as is that terrible night of contemplation which we are to describe, into which, of set purpose, God brings the soul that He may lead it to Divine union.

2. This sweetness, then, and this interior pleasure which we are describing, and which these progressives find and experience in their spirits so easily and so abundantly, is communicated to them in much greater abundance than aforetime, overflowing into their senses more than was usual previously to this purgation of sense; for, inasmuch as the sense is now purer, it can more easily feel the pleasures of the spirit after its manner. As, however, this sensual part of the soul is weak and incapable of experiencing the strong things of the spirit, it follows that these proficients, by reason of this spiritual communication which is made to their sensual part, endure therein many frailties and sufferings and weaknesses of the stomach, and in consequence are fatigued in spirit. For, as the Wise Man says: "The corruptible body presseth down the soul."[2] Hence comes it that the communications that are granted to these souls cannot be very strong or very intense or very spiritual, as is required for Divine union with God, by reason of the weakness and corruption of the sensual nature which has a part in them. Hence arise the raptures and trances and dislocations of the bones which always happen when the communications are not purely spiritual—that is, are not given to the spirit alone, as are those of the perfect who are purified by the second night of the spirit, and in whom these raptures and torments of the body no longer exist, since they are enjoying liberty of spirit, and their senses are now neither clouded nor transported.

3. And in order that the necessity for such souls to enter this night of the spirit may be understood, we will here note certain imperfections and perils which belong to these proficients.

---

[1] Psalm cxlvii, 17.
[2] Wisdom ix, 15.

CHAPTER II

Describes other imperfections which belong to these proficients.

THESE PROFICIENTS have two kinds of imperfection: the one kind is habitual; the other actual. The habitual imperfections are the imperfect habits and affections which have remained all the time in the spirit, and are like roots, to which the purgation of sense has been unable to penetrate. The difference between the purgation of these and that of this other kind is the difference between the root and the branch, or between the removing of a stain which is fresh and one which is old and of long standing. For, as we said, the purgation of sense is only the entrance and beginning of contemplation leading to the purgation of the spirit, which, as we have likewise said, serves rather to accommodate sense to spirit than to unite spirit with God. But there still remain in the spirit the stains of the old man, although the spirit thinks not that this is so, neither can it perceive them; if these stains be not removed with the soap and strong lye of the purgation of this night, the spirit will be unable to come to the purity of Divine union.

2. These souls have likewise the *hebetudo mentis*[1] and the natural roughness which every man contracts through sin, and the distraction and outward clinging of the spirit, which must be enlightened, refined and recollected by the afflictions and perils of that night. These habitual imperfections belong to all those who have not passed beyond this state of the proficient; they cannot coexist, as we say, with the perfect state of union through love.

3. To actual imperfections all are not liable in the same way. Some, whose spiritual good is so superficial and so readily affected by sense, fall into greater difficulties and dangers, which we described at the beginning of this treatise. For, as they find so many and such abundant spiritual communications and apprehensions, both in sense and in spirit, wherein they oftentimes see imaginary and spiritual visions (for all these things, together with other delectable feelings, come to many souls in this state, wherein the devil and their own fancy very commonly practice deceptions on them), and, as the devil is apt to take such pleasure in impressing upon the soul and suggesting to it the said apprehensions and feelings, he fascinates and deludes it with great ease, unless it takes the precaution of resigning itself to God, and of protecting itself strongly, by means of faith, from all these visions and feelings. For in this state the

---

[1] ["deadening of the mind."]

devil causes many to believe in vain visions and false prophecies; and strives to make them presume that God and the saints are speaking with them; and they often trust their own fancy. And the devil is also accustomed, in this state, to fill them with presumption and pride, so that they become attracted by vanity and arrogance, and allow themselves to be seen engaging in outward acts which appear holy, such as raptures and other manifestations. Thus they become bold with God, and lose holy fear, which is the key and the custodian of all the virtues; and in some of these souls so many are the falsehoods and deceits which tend to multiply, and so inveterate do they grow, that it is very doubtful if such souls will return to the pure road of virtue and true spirituality. Into these miseries they fall because they are beginning to give themselves over to spiritual feelings and apprehensions with too great security, when they were beginning to make some progress upon the way.

4. There is much more that I might say of these imperfections and of how they are the more incurable because such souls consider them to be more spiritual than the others, but I will leave this subject. I shall only add, in order to prove how necessary, for him that would go farther, is the night of the spirit, which is purgation, that none of these proficients, however strenuously he may have labored, is free, at best, from many of those natural affections and imperfect habits, purification from which, we said, is necessary if a soul is to pass to Divine union.

5. And over and above this (as we have said already), inasmuch as the lower part of the soul still has a share in these spiritual communications, they cannot be as intense, as pure and as strong as is needful for the aforesaid union; wherefore, in order to come to this union, the soul must needs enter into the second night of the spirit, wherein it must strip sense and spirit perfectly from all these apprehensions and from all sweetness, and be made to walk in dark and pure faith, which is the proper and adequate means whereby the soul is united with God, according as Osee says, in these words: "I will betroth thee—that is, I will unite thee—with Me through faith."[2]

CHAPTER III

Annotation for that which follows.

THESE souls, then, have now become proficients, because of the time which they have spent in feeding the senses with sweet communications,

[2] Osee ii, 20.

so that their sensual part, being thus attracted and delighted by spiritual pleasure, which came to it from the spirit, may be united with the spirit and made one with it; each part after its own manner eating of one and the same spiritual food and from one and the same dish, as one person and with one sole intent, so that thus they may in a certain way be united and brought into agreement, and, thus united, may be prepared for the endurance of the stern and severe purgation of the spirit which awaits them. In this purgation these two parts of the soul, the spiritual and the sensual, must be completely purged, since the one is never truly purged without the other, the purgation of sense becoming effective when that of the spirit has fairly begun. Wherefore the night which we have called that of sense may and should be called a kind of correction and restraint of the desire rather than purgation. The reason is that all the imperfections and disorders of the sensual part have their strength and root in the spirit, where all habits, both good and bad, are brought into subjection, and thus, until these are purged, the rebellions and depravities of sense cannot be purged thoroughly.

2. Wherefore, in this night following, both parts of the soul are purged together, and it is for this end that it is well to have passed through the corrections of the first night, and the period of tranquillity which proceeds from it, in order that, sense being united with spirit, both may be purged after a certain manner and may then suffer with greater fortitude. For very great fortitude is needful for so violent and severe a purgation, since, if the weakness of the lower part has not first been corrected and fortitude has not been gained from God through the sweet and delectable communion which the soul has afterwards enjoyed with Him, its nature will not have the strength or the disposition to bear it.

3. Therefore, since these proficients are still at a very low stage of progress, and follow their own nature closely in the intercourse and dealings which they have with God, because the gold of their spirit is not yet purified and refined, they still think of God as little children, and speak of God as little children, and feel and experience God as little children, even as Saint Paul says,[1] because they have not reached perfection, which is the union of the soul with God. In the state of union, however, they will work great things in the spirit, even as grown men, and their works and faculties will then be Divine rather than human, as will afterwards be said. To this end God is pleased to strip them of this old man and clothe them with the new man, who is created according to God, as the Apostle says,[2] in the newness of sense. He

---

[1] 1 Corinthians xiii, 11.
[2] [Ephesians iv, 24.]

strips their faculties, affections and feelings, both spiritual and sensual, both outward and inward, leaving the understanding dark, the will dry, the memory empty and the affections in the deepest affliction, bitterness and constraint, taking from the soul the pleasure and experience of spiritual blessings which it had aforetime, in order to make of this privation one of the principles which are requisite in the spirit so that there may be introduced into it and united with it the spiritual form of the spirit, which is the union of love. All this the Lord works in the soul by means of a pure and dark contemplation, as the soul explains in the first stanza. This, although we originally interpreted it with reference to the first night of sense, is principally understood by the soul of this second night of the spirit, since this is the principal part of the purification of the soul. And thus we shall set it down and expound it here again in this sense.

CHAPTER IV

Sets down the first stanza and the exposition thereof.

On a dark night,   Kindled in love with yearnings—oh, happy chance!— I went forth without being observed,   My house being now at rest.

EXPOSITION

INTERPRETING THIS stanza now with reference to purgation, contemplation or detachment or poverty of spirit, which here are almost one and the same thing, we can expound it after this manner and make the soul speak thus: In poverty, and without protection or support in all the apprehensions of my soul—that is, in the darkness of my understanding and the constraint of my will, in affliction and anguish with respect to memory, remaining in the dark in pure faith, which is dark night for the said natural faculties, the will alone being touched by grief and afflictions and yearnings for the love of God—I went forth from myself—that is, from my low manner of understanding, from my weak mode of loving and from my poor and limited manner of experiencing God, without being hindered therein by sensuality or the devil.

2. This was a great happiness and a good chance for me; for, when the faculties had been perfectly annihilated and calmed, together with the passions, desires and affections of my soul, wherewith I had experienced and tasted God after a lowly manner, I went forth from my own human dealings and operations to the operations and dealings of God. That is to say, my understanding went forth from itself, turning from the human

and natural to the Divine; for, when it is united with God by means of this purgation, its understanding no longer comes through its natural light and vigour, but through the Divine Wisdom wherewith it has become united. And my will went forth from itself, becoming Divine; for, being united with Divine love, it no longer loves with its natural strength after a lowly manner, but with strength and purity from the Holy Spirit; and thus the will, which is now near to God, acts not after a human manner, and similarly the memory has become transformed into eternal apprehensions of glory. And finally, by means of this night and purgation of the old man, all the energies and affections of the soul are wholly renewed into a Divine temper and Divine delight.

There follows the line:

On a dark night.

CHAPTER V

Sets down the first line and begins to explain how this dark contemplation is not only night for the soul but is also grief and torment.

THIS DARK night is an inflowing of God into the soul, which purges it from its ignorances and imperfections, habitual, natural and spiritual, and which is called by contemplatives infused contemplation, or mystical theology. Herein God secretly teaches the soul and instructs it in perfection of love, without its doing anything, or understanding of what manner is this infused contemplation. Inasmuch as it is the loving wisdom of God, God produces striking effects in the soul, for, by purging and illumining it, He prepares it for the union of love with God. Wherefore the same loving wisdom that purges the blessed spirits and enlightens them is that which here purges the soul and illumines it.

2. But the question arises: Why is the Divine light (which, as we say, illumines and purges the soul from its ignorances) here called by the soul a dark night? To this the answer is that for two reasons this Divine wisdom is not only night and darkness for the soul, but is likewise affliction and torment. The first is because of the height of Divine Wisdom, which transcends the talent of the soul, and in this way is darkness to it; the second, because of its vileness and impurity, in which respect it is painful and afflictive to it, and is also dark.

3. In order to prove the first point, we must here assume a certain doctrine of the philosopher, which says that, the clearer and more manifest are Divine things in themselves, the darker and more hidden are

they to the soul naturally; just as, the clearer is the light, the more it
blinds and darkens the pupil of the owl, and, the more directly we look
at the sun, the greater is the darkness which it causes in our visual faculty, overcoming and overwhelming it through its own weakness. In the
same way, when this Divine light of contemplation assails the soul which
is not yet wholly enlightened, it causes spiritual darkness in it; for not
only does it overcome it, but likewise it overwhelms it and darkens the
act of its natural intelligence. For this reason Saint Dionysius and other
mystical theologians call this infused contemplation a ray of darkness—
that is to say, for the soul that is not enlightened and purged—for the natural strength of the intellect is transcended and overwhelmed by its great
supernatural light. Wherefore David likewise said: That near to God and
round about Him are darkness and cloud;[1] not that this is so in fact, but
that it is so to our weak understanding, which is blinded and darkened
by so vast a light, to which it cannot attain. For this cause the same David
then explained himself, saying: "Through the great splendour of His
presence passed clouds"[2]—that is, between God and our understanding.
And it is for this cause that, when God sends it out from Himself to the
soul that is not yet transformed, this illumining ray of His secret wisdom
causes thick darkness in the understanding.

4. And it is clear that this dark contemplation is in these its beginnings painful likewise to the soul; for, as this Divine infused contemplation has many excellences that are extremely good, and the soul that
receives them, not being purged, has many miseries that are likewise
extremely bad, hence it follows that, as two contraries cannot coexist in
one subject—the soul—it must of necessity have pain and suffering,
since it is the subject wherein these two contraries war against each
other, working the one against the other, by reason of the purgation of
the imperfections of the soul which comes to pass through this contemplation. This we shall prove inductively in the manner following.

5. In the first place, because the light and wisdom of this contemplation is most bright and pure, and the soul which it assails is dark and
impure, it follows that the soul suffers great pain when it receives it in
itself, just as, when the eyes are dimmed by humors, and become
impure and weak, the assault made upon them by a bright light causes
them pain. And when the soul suffers the direct assault of this Divine
light, its pain, which results from its impurity, is immense; because,
when this pure light assails the soul, in order to expel its impurity, the
soul feels itself to be so impure and miserable that it believes God to be

---

[1] Psalm xcvii, 2
[2] Psalm xviii, 12.

against it, and thinks that it has set itself up against God. This causes it
sore grief and pain, because it now believes that God has cast it away:
this was one of the greatest trials which Job felt when God sent him this
experience, and he said: "Why hast Thou set me contrary to Thee, so
that I am grievous and burdensome to myself?"[3] For, by means of this
pure light, the soul now sees its impurity clearly (although darkly), and
knows clearly that it is unworthy of God or of any creature. And what
gives it most pain is that it thinks that it will never be worthy and that
its good things are all over for it. This is caused by the profound immer-
sion of its spirit in the knowledge and realization of its evils and miseries; for this Divine and dark light now reveals them all to the eye, that
it may see clearly how in its own strength it can never have aught else.
In this sense we may understand that passage from David, which says:
"For iniquity Thou hast corrected man and hast made his soul to be
undone and consumed: he wastes away as the spider."[4]

6. The second way in which the soul suffers pain is by reason of its
weakness, natural, moral and spiritual; for, when this Divine contemplation assails the soul with a certain force, in order to strengthen it and
subdue it, it suffers such pain in its weakness that it nearly swoons away.
This is especially so at certain times when it is assailed with somewhat
greater force; for sense and spirit, as if beneath some immense and dark
load, are in such great pain and agony that the soul would find advantage and relief in death. This had been experienced by the prophet Job,
when he said: "I desire not that He should have intercourse with me in
great strength, lest He oppress me with the weight of His greatness."[5]

7. Beneath the power of this oppression and weight the soul feels
itself so far from being favored that it thinks, and correctly so, that even
that wherein it was wont to find some help has vanished with everything else, and that there is none who has pity upon it. To this effect
Job says likewise: "Have pity upon me, have pity upon me, at least ye
my friends, because the hand of the Lord has touched me."[6] A thing of
great wonder and pity is it that the soul's weakness and impurity should
now be so great that, though the hand of God is of itself so light and
gentle, the soul should now feel it to be so heavy and so contrary,
though it neither weighs it down nor rests upon it, but only touches it,
and that mercifully, since He does this in order to grant the soul favors
and not to chastise it.

---

[3] Job vii, 20.
[4] Psalm xxxix, 11.
[5] Job xxiii, 6.
[6] Job xix, 21.

CHAPTER VI

Of other kinds of pain that the soul suffers in this night.

THE THIRD kind of suffering and pain that the soul endures in this state results from the fact that two other extremes meet here in one, namely, the Divine and the human. The Divine is this purgative contemplation, and the human is the subject—that is, the soul. The Divine assails the soul in order to renew it and thus to make it Divine; and, stripping it of the habitual affections and attachments of the old man, to which it is very closely united, knit together and conformed, destroys and consumes its spiritual substance, and absorbs it in deep and profound darkness. As a result of this, the soul feels itself to be perishing and melting away, in the presence and sight of its miseries, in a cruel spiritual death, even as if it had been swallowed by a beast and felt itself being devoured in the darkness of its belly, suffering such anguish as was endured by Jonas in the belly of that beast of the sea.[1] For in this sepulchre of dark death it must needs abide until the spiritual resurrection which it hopes for.

2. A description of this suffering and pain, although in truth it transcends all description, is given by David, when he says: "The lamentations of death compassed me about; the pains of hell surrounded me; I cried in my tribulation."[2] But what the sorrowful soul feels most in this condition is its clear perception, as it thinks, that God has abandoned it, and, in His abhorrence of it, has flung it into darkness; it is a grave and piteous grief for it to believe that God has forsaken it. It is this that David also felt so much in a like case, saying: "After the manner wherein the wounded are dead in the sepulchres, being now cast off by Thy hand, so that Thou rememberest them no more, even so have they set me in the deepest and lowest lake, in the dark places and in the shadow of death, and Thy fury is confirmed upon me and all Thy waves Thou hast brought in upon me."[3] For indeed, when this purgative contemplation is most severe, the soul feels very keenly the shadow of death and the lamentations of death and the pains of hell, which consist in its feeling itself to be without God, and chastised and cast out, and unworthy of Him; and it feels that He is wroth with it. All this is felt by the soul in this condition—yea, and more, for it believes that it is so with it for ever.

3. It feels, too, that all creatures have forsaken it, and that it is contemned

---

[1] Jonas ii, I.
[2] Psalm xvii, 5–7.
[3] Psalm lxxxviii, 5–7.

by them, particularly by its friends. Wherefore David presently continues, saying: "Thou hast put far from me my friends and acquaintances; they have counted me an abomination."[4] To all this will Jonas testify, as one who likewise experienced it in the belly of the beast, both bodily and spiritually. "Thou hast cast me forth (he says) into the deep, into the heart of the sea, and the flood hath compassed me; all its billows and waves have passed over me. And I said, 'I am cast away out of the sight of Thine eyes, but I shall once again see Thy holy temple' (which he says, because God purifies the soul in this state that it may see His temple); the waters compassed me, even to the soul, the deep hath closed me round about, the ocean hath covered my head; I went down to the lowest parts of the mountains; the bars of the earth have shut me up for ever."[5] By these bars are here understood, in this sense, imperfections of the soul, which have impeded it from enjoying this delectable contemplation.

4. The fourth kind of pain is caused in the soul by another excellence of this dark contemplation, which is its majesty and greatness, from which arises in the soul a consciousness of the other extreme which is in itself—namely, that of the deepest poverty and wretchedness: this is one of the chiefest pains that it suffers in this purgation. For it feels within itself a profound emptiness and impoverishment of three kinds of good, which are ordained for the pleasure of the soul, which are the temporal, the natural and the spiritual; and finds itself set in the midst of the evils contrary to these, namely, miseries of imperfection, aridity and emptiness of the apprehensions of the faculties and abandonment of the spirit in darkness. Inasmuch as God here purges the soul according to the substance of its sense and spirit, and according to the interior and exterior faculties, the soul must needs be in all its parts reduced to a state of emptiness, poverty and abandonment and must be left dry and empty and in darkness. For the sensual part is purified in aridity, the faculties are purified in the emptiness of their perceptions and the spirit is purified in thick darkness.

5. All this God brings to pass by means of this dark contemplation; wherein the soul not only suffers this emptiness and the suspension of these natural supports and perceptions, which is a most afflictive suffering (as if a man were suspended or held in the air so that he could not breathe), but likewise He is purging the soul, annihilating it, emptying it or consuming in it (even as fire consumes the mouldiness and the rust of metal) all the affections and imperfect habits which it has contracted in its whole life. Since these are deeply rooted in the

---

[4] Psalm lxxxviii, 8.
[5] Jonas ii, 3–6.

substance of the soul, it is wont to suffer great undoing and inward torment, besides the said poverty and emptiness, natural and spiritual, so that there may here be fulfilled that passage from Ezechiel which says: "Heap together the bones and I will burn them in the fire; the flesh shall be consumed and the whole composition shall be burned and the bones shall be destroyed."[6] Herein is understood the pain which is suffered in the emptiness and poverty of the substance of the soul both in sense and in spirit. And concerning this he then says: "Set it also empty upon the coals, that its metal may become hot and molten, and its uncleanness may be destroyed within it, and its rust may be consumed."[7] Herein is described the grave suffering which the soul here endures in the purgation of the fire of this contemplation, for the Prophet says here that, in order for the rust of the affections which are within the soul to be purified and destroyed, it is needful that, in a certain manner, the soul itself should be annihilated and destroyed, since these passions and imperfections have become natural to it.

6. Wherefore, because the soul is purified in this furnace like gold in a crucible, as says the Wise Man,[8] it is conscious of this complete undoing of itself in its very substance, together with the direst poverty, wherein it is, as it were, nearing its end, as may be seen by that which David says of himself in this respect, in these words: "Save me, Lord (he cries to God), for the waters have come in even unto my soul; I am made fast in the mire of the deep and there is no place where I can stand; I am come into the depth of the sea and a tempest hath overwhelmed me; I have labored crying, my throat has become hoarse, mine eyes have failed whilst I hope in my God."[9] Here God greatly humbles the soul in order that He may afterwards greatly exalt it; and if He ordained not that, when these feelings arise within the soul, they should speedily be stilled, it would die in a very short space; but there are only occasional periods when it is conscious of their greatest intensity. At times, however, they are so keen that the soul seems to be seeing hell and perdition opened. Of such are they that in truth go down alive into hell, being purged here on earth in the same manner as there, since this purgation is that which would have to be accomplished there. And thus the soul that passes through this either enters not that place[10] at all, or tarries there but for a very short time; for one hour of purgation here is more profitable than are many there.

---

[6] Ezechiel xxiv 10.
[7] Ezechiel xxiv, II.
[8] Wisdom iii, 6.
[9] Psalm lxix , 1–3.
[10] [i.e., purgatory.]

CHAPTER VII

Continues the same matter and considers other afflictions and constraints of the will.

THE AFFLICTIONS and constraints of the will are now very great likewise, and of such a kind that they sometimes transpierce the soul with a sudden remembrance of the evils in the midst of which it finds itself, and with the uncertainty of finding a remedy for them. And to this is added the remembrance of times of prosperity now past; for as a rule souls that enter this night have had many consolations from God, and have rendered Him many services, and it causes them the greater grief to see that they are far removed from that happiness, and unable to enter into it. This was also described by Job, who had had experience of it, in these words: "I, who was wont to be wealthy and rich, am suddenly undone and broken to pieces; He hath taken me by my neck; He hath broken me and set me up for His mark to wound me; He hath compassed me round about with His lances; He hath wounded all my loins; He hath not spared; He hath poured out my bowels on the earth; He hath broken me with wound upon wound; He hath assailed me as a strong giant; I have sewed sackcloth upon my skin and have covered my flesh with ashes; my face is become swollen with weeping and mine eyes are blinded."[1]

2. So many and so grievous are the afflictions of this night, and so many passages of Scripture are there which could be cited to this purpose, that time and strength would fail us to write of them, for all that can be said thereof is certainly less than the truth. From the passages already quoted some idea may be gained of them. And, that we may bring the exposition of this line to a close and explain more fully what is worked in the soul by this night, I shall tell what Jeremias felt about it, which, since there is so much of it, he describes and bewails in many words after this manner: "I am the man that see my poverty in the rod of His indignation; He hath threatened me and brought me into darkness and not into light. So far hath He turned against me and hath converted His hand upon me all the day! My skin and my flesh hath He made old; He hath broken my bones; He hath made a fence around me and compassed me with gall and trial; He hath set me in dark places, as those that are dead for ever. He hath made a fence around me and against me, that I may not go out; He hath made my captivity heavy. Yea, and when I have cried and have entreated, He hath shut out my prayer. He hath enclosed my paths and ways out with square stones; He hath thwarted my steps. He hath set

---

[1] Job xvi, 12–16.

ambushes for me; He hath become to me a lion in a secret place. He hath turned aside my steps and broken me in pieces, He hath made me desolate; He hath bent His bow and set me as a mark for His arrow. He hath shot into my reins the daughters of His quiver. I have become a derision to all the people, and laughter and scorn for them all the day. He hath filled me with bitterness and hath made me drunken with wormwood. He hath broken my teeth by number; He hath fed me with ashes. My soul is cast out from peace; I have forgotten good things. And I said: 'Mine end is frustrated and cut short, together with my desire and my hope from the Lord. Remember my poverty and my excess, the wormwood and the gall. I shall be mindful with remembrance and my soul shall be undone within me in pains.'"[2]

3. All these complaints Jeremias makes about these pains and trials, and by means of them he most vividly depicts the sufferings of the soul in this spiritual night and purgation. Wherefore the soul that God sets in this tempestuous and horrible night is deserving of great compassion. For, although it experiences much happiness by reason of the great blessings that must arise on this account within it, when, as Job says, God raises up profound blessings in the soul out of darkness, and brings up to light the shadow of death,[3] so that, as David says, His light comes to be as was His darkness;[4] yet notwithstanding, by reason of the dreadful pain which the soul is suffering, and of the great uncertainty which it has concerning the remedy for it, since it believes, as this prophet says here, that its evil will never end, and it thinks, as David says likewise, that God set it in dark places like those that are dead, and for this reason brought its spirit within it into anguish and troubled its heart,[5] it suffers great pain and grief, since there is added to all this (because of the solitude and abandonment caused in it by this dark night) the fact that it finds no consolation or support in any instruction nor in a spiritual master. For, although in many ways its director may show it good reason for being comforted because of the blessings which are contained in these afflictions, it cannot believe him. For it is so greatly absorbed and immersed in the realization of those evils wherein it sees its own miseries so clearly, that it thinks that, as its director observes not that which it sees and feels, he is speaking in this manner because he understands it not; and so, instead of comfort, it rather receives fresh affliction, since it believes that its director's advice con-

---

[2] Lamentations iii, 1–20.
[3] Job xii, 22.
[4] Psalm cxxxix, 12.
[5] Psalm cxliii, 3–4.

tains no remedy for its troubles. And, in truth, this is so; for, until the Lord shall have completely purged it after the manner that He wills, no means or remedy is of any service or profit for the relief of its affliction; the more so because the soul is as powerless in this case as one who has been imprisoned in a dark dungeon, and is bound hand and foot, and can neither move nor see, nor feel any favor whether from above or from below, until the spirit is humbled, softened and purified, and grows so keen and delicate and pure that it can become one with the Spirit of God, according to the degree of union of love which His mercy is pleased to grant it; in proportion to this the purgation is of greater or less severity and of greater or less duration.

4. But, if it is to be really effectual, it will last for some years, however severe it be; since the purgative process allows intervals of relief, wherein, by the dispensation of God, this dark contemplation ceases to assail the soul in the form and manner of purgation, and assails it after an illuminative and a loving manner, wherein the soul, like one that has gone forth from this dungeon and imprisonment, and is brought into the recreation of spaciousness and liberty, feels and experiences great sweetness of peace and loving friendship with God, together with a ready abundance of spiritual communication. This is to the soul a sign of the health which is being wrought within it by the said purgation and a foretaste of the abundance for which it hopes. Occasionally this is so great that the soul believes its trials to be at last over. For spiritual things in the soul, when they are most purely spiritual, have this characteristic that, if trials come to it, the soul believes that it will never escape from them, and that all its blessings are now over, as has been seen in the passages quoted; and, if spiritual blessings come, the soul believes in the same way that its troubles are now over, and that blessings will never fail it. This was so with David, when he found himself in the midst of them, as he confesses in these words: "I said in my abundance: 'I shall never be moved.'"[6]

5. This happens because the actual possession by the spirit of one of two contrary things itself makes impossible the actual possession and realization of the other contrary thing; this is not so, however, in the sensual part of the soul, because its apprehension is weak. But, as the spirit is not yet completely purged and cleansed from the affections that it has contracted from its lower part, while changing not in so far as it is spirit, it can be moved to further afflictions in so far as these affections sway it. In this way, as we see, David was afterwards moved, and

---

[6] Psalm xxx, 6.

experienced many ills and afflictions, although in the time of his abundance he had thought and said that he would never be moved. Just so is it with the soul in this condition, when it sees itself moved by that abundance of spiritual blessings, and, being unable to see the root of the imperfection and impurity which still remain within it, thinks that its trials are over.

6. This thought, however, comes to the soul but seldom, for, until spiritual purification is complete and perfected, the sweet communication is very rarely so abundant as to conceal from the soul the root which remains hidden, in such a way that the soul can cease to feel that there is something that it lacks within itself or that it has still to do. Thus it cannot completely enjoy that relief, but feels as if one of its enemies were within it, and although this enemy is, as it were, hushed and asleep, it fears that he will come to life again and attack it. And this is what indeed happens, for, when the soul is most secure and least alert, it is dragged down and immersed again in another and a worse degree of affliction which is severer and darker and more grievous than that which is past; and this new affliction will continue for a further period of time, perhaps longer than the first. And the soul once more comes to believe that all its blessings are over for ever. Although it had thought during its first trial that there were no more afflictions which it could suffer, and yet, after the trial was over, it enjoyed great blessings, this experience is not sufficient to take away its belief, during this second degree of trial, that all is now over for it and that it will never again be happy as in the past. For, as I say, this belief, of which the soul is so sure, is caused in it by the actual apprehension of the spirit, which annihilates within it all that is contrary to it.

7. This is the reason why those who lie in purgatory suffer great misgivings as to whether they will ever go forth from it and whether their pains will ever be over. For, although they have the habit of the three theological virtues—faith, hope and charity—the present realization which they have of their afflictions and of their deprivation of God allows them not to enjoy the present blessing and consolation of these virtues. For, although they are able to realize that they have a great love for God, this is no consolation to them, since they cannot think that God loves them or that they are worthy that He should do so; rather, as they see that they are deprived of Him, and left in their own miseries, they think that there is that in themselves which provides a very good reason why they should with perfect justice be abhorred and cast out by God for ever. And thus, although the soul in this purgation is conscious that it has a great love for God and would give a thousand lives for Him (which is the truth, for in these trials such souls love their God very earnestly), yet this is no relief to it, but rather brings it greater

affliction. For it loves Him so much that it cares about naught beside; when, therefore, it sees itself to be so wretched that it cannot believe that God loves it, nor that there is or will ever be reason why He should do so, but rather that there is reason why it should be abhorred, not only by Him, but by all creatures for ever, it is grieved to see in itself reasons for deserving to be cast out by Him for Whom it has such great love and desire.

CHAPTER VIII

Of other pains which afflict the soul in this state.

BUT THERE is another thing here that afflicts and distresses the soul greatly, which is that, as this dark night has hindered its faculties and affections in this way, it is unable to raise its affection or its mind to God, neither can it pray to Him, thinking, as Jeremias thought concerning himself, that God has set a cloud before it through which its prayer cannot pass.[1] For it is this that is meant by that which is said in the passage referred to, namely: "He hath shut and enclosed my paths with square stones."[2] And if it sometimes prays it does so with such lack of strength and of sweetness that it thinks that God neither hears it nor pays heed to it, as this Prophet likewise declares in the same passage, saying: "When I cry and entreat, He hath shut out my prayer."[3] In truth this is no time for the soul to speak with God; it should rather put its mouth in the dust, as Jeremias says, so that perchance there may come to it some present hope,[4] and it may endure its purgation with patience. It is God Who is passively working here in the soul; wherefore the soul can do nothing. Hence it can neither pray nor pay attention when it is present at the Divine offices, much less can it attend to other things and affairs which are temporal. Not only so, but it has likewise such distractions and times of such profound forgetfulness of the memory that frequent periods pass by without its knowing what it has been doing or thinking, or what it is that it is doing or is going to do, neither can it pay attention, although it desire to do so, to anything that occupies it.

2. Inasmuch as not only is the understanding here purged of its light,

---

[1] Lamentations iii, 44.
[2] [Lamentations iii, 9.]
[3] Lamentations iii, 8.
[4] Lamentations, iii, 29.

and the will of its affections, but the memory is also purged of meditation and knowledge, it is well that it be likewise annihilated with
respect to all these things, so that that which David says of himself in
this purgation may by fulfilled, namely: "I was annihilated and I knew
not."[5] This unknowing refers to these follies and forgetfulnesses of the
memory, which distractions and forgetfulnesses are caused by the interior recollection wherein this contemplation absorbs the soul. For, in
order that the soul may be divinely prepared and tempered with its faculties for the Divine union of love, it would be well for it to be first of
all absorbed, with all its faculties, in this Divine and dark spiritual light
of contemplation, and thus to be withdrawn from all the affections and
apprehensions of the creatures, which condition ordinarily continues
in proportion to its intensity. And thus, the simpler and the purer is this
Divine light in its assault upon the soul, the more does it darken it, void
it and annihilate it according to its particular apprehensions and affections, with regard both to things above and to things below; and similarly, the less simple and pure is it in this assault, the less deprivation it
causes it and the less dark is it. Now this is a thing that seems incredi-
ble, to say that, the brighter and purer is supernatural and Divine light,
the more it darkens the soul, and that, the less bright and pure is it, the
less dark it is to the soul. Yet this may readily be understood if we
consider what has been proved above by the dictum of the philosopher—namely, that the brighter and the more manifest in themselves
are supernatural things the darker are they to our understanding.

3. And, to the end that this may be understood the more clearly, we
shall here set down a similitude referring to common and natural light.
We observe that a ray of sunlight which enters through the window is
the less clearly visible according as it is the purer and freer from specks,
and the more of such specks and motes there are in the air, the brighter
is the light to the eye. The reason is that it is not the light itself that is
seen; the light is but the means whereby the other things that it strikes
are seen, and then it is also seen itself, through its reflection in them;
were it not for this, neither it nor they would have been seen. Thus if
the ray of sunlight entered through the window of one room and passed
out through another on the other side, traversing the room, and if it
met nothing on the way, or if there were no specks in the air for it to
strike, the room would have no more light than before, neither would
the ray of light be visible. In fact, if we consider it carefully, there is
more darkness where the ray is, since it absorbs and obscures any other

---

[5] Psalm lxxiii, 22.

light, and yet it is itself invisible, because, as we have said, there are no visible objects which it can strike.

4. Now this is precisely what this Divine ray of contemplation does in the soul. Assailing it with its Divine light, it transcends the natural power of the soul, and herein it darkens it and deprives it of all natural affections and apprehensions which it apprehended aforetime by means of natural light; and thus it leaves it not only dark, but likewise empty, according to its faculties and desires, both spiritual and natural. And, by thus leaving it empty and in darkness, it purges and illumines it with Divine spiritual light, although the soul thinks not that it has this light, but believes itself to be in darkness, even as we have said of the ray of light, which, although it be in the midst of the room, yet, if it be pure and meet nothing on its path, is not visible. With regard, however, to this spiritual light by which the soul is assailed, when it has something to strike—that is, when something spiritual presents itself to be understood, however small a speck it be and whether of perfection or imperfection, or whether it be a judgment of the falsehood or the truth of a thing—it then sees and understands much more clearly than before it was in these dark places. And exactly in the same way it discerns the spiritual light which it has in order that it may readily discern the imperfection which is presented to it; even as, when the ray of which we have spoken, within the room, is dark and not itself visible, if one introduce a hand or any other thing into its path, the hand is then seen and it is realized that that sunlight is present.

5. Wherefore, since this spiritual light is so simple, pure and general, not appropriated or restricted to any particular thing that can be understood, whether natural or Divine (since with respect to all these apprehensions the faculties of the soul are empty and annihilated), it follows that with great comprehensiveness and readiness the soul discerns and penetrates whatsoever thing presents itself to it, whether it come from above or from below; for which cause the Apostle said: That the spiritual man searches all things, even the deep things of God.[6] For by this general and simple wisdom is understood that which the Holy Spirit says through the Wise Man, namely: That it reaches wheresoever it wills by reason of its purity;[7] that is to say, because it is not restricted to any particular object of the intellect or affection. And this is the characteristic of the spirit that is purged and annihilated with respect to all particular affections and objects of the understanding, that in this state

---

[6] 1 Corinthians ii, 10.
[7] Wisdom vii, 24.

wherein it has pleasure in nothing and understands nothing in particular, but dwells in its emptiness, darkness and obscurity, it is fully prepared to embrace everything to the end that those words of Saint Paul may be fulfilled in it: *Nihil habentes, et omnia possidentes*.[8] For such poverty of spirit as this would deserve such happiness.

CHAPTER IX

How, although this night brings darkness to the spirit, it does so in order to illumine it and give it light.

IT NOW remains to be said that, although this happy night brings darkness to the spirit, it does so only to give it light in everything; and that, although it humbles it and makes it miserable, it does so only to exalt it and to raise it up; and, although it impoverishes it and empties it of all natural affection and attachment, it does so only that it may enable it to stretch forward, divinely, and thus to have fruition and experience of all things, both above and below, yet to preserve its unrestricted liberty of spirit in them all. For just as the elements, in order that they may have a part in all natural entities and compounds, must have no particular color, odor or taste, so as to be able to combine with all tastes odors and colors, just so must the spirit be simple, pure and detached from all kinds of natural affection, whether actual or habitual, to the end that it may be able freely to share in the breadth of spirit of the Divine Wisdom, wherein, through its purity, it has experience of all the sweetness of all things in a certain pre-eminently excellent way. And without this purgation it will be wholly unable to feel or experience the satisfaction of all this abundance of spiritual sweetness. For one single affection remaining in the spirit, or one particular thing to which, actually or habitually, it clings, suffices to hinder it from feeling or experiencing or communicating the delicacy and intimate sweetness of the spirit of love, which contains within itself all sweetness to a most eminent degree.

2. For, even as the children of Israel, solely because they retained one single affection and remembrance—namely, with respect to the fleshpots and the meals which they had tasted in Egypt[1]—could not

---

[8] 2 Corinthians vi, 10.

---

[1] Exodus xvi, 3.

relish the delicate bread of angels, in the desert, which was the manna, which, as the Divine Scripture says, held sweetness for every taste and turned to the taste that each one desired;[2] even so the spirit cannot succeed in enjoying the delights of the spirit of liberty, according to the desire of the will, if it be still affectioned to any desire, whether actual or habitual, or to particular objects of understanding, or to any other apprehension. The reason for this is that the affections, feelings and apprehensions of the perfect spirit, being Divine, are of another kind and of a very different order from those that are natural. They are pre-eminent, so that, in order both actually and habitually to possess the one, it is needful to expel and annihilate the other, as with two contrary things, which cannot exist together in one person. Therefore it is most fitting and necessary, if the soul is to pass to these great things, that this dark night of contemplation should first of all annihilate and undo it in its meannesses, bringing it into darkness, aridity, affliction and emptiness; for the light which is to be given to it is a Divine light of the highest kind, which transcends all natural light, and which by nature can find no place in the understanding.

3. And thus it is fitting that, if the understanding is to be united with that light and become Divine in the state of perfection, it should first of all be purged and annihilated as to its natural light, and, by means of this dark contemplation, be brought actually into darkness. This darkness should continue for as long as is needful in order to expel and annihilate the habit which the soul has long since formed in its manner of understanding, and the Divine light and illumination will then take its place. And thus, inasmuch as that power of understanding which it had aforetime is natural, it follows that the darkness which it here suffers is profound and horrible and most painful, for this darkness, being felt in the deepest substance of the spirit, seems to be substantial darkness. Similarly, since the affection of love which is to be given to it in the Divine union of love is Divine, and therefore very spiritual, subtle and delicate, and very intimate, transcending every affection and feeling of the will, and every desire thereof, it is fitting that, in order that the will may be able to attain to this Divine affection and most lofty delight, and to feel it and experience it through the union of love, since it is not, in the way of nature, perceptible to the will, it be first of all purged and annihilated in all its affections and feelings, and left in a condition of aridity and constraint, proportionate to the habit of natural affections which it had before, with respect both to Divine things and to human.

---

[2] Wisdom, xvi, 21.

Thus, being exhausted, withered and thoroughly tried in the fire of this dark contemplation, and having driven away every kind of evil spirit (as with the heart of the fish which Tobias set on the coals[3]), it may have a simple and pure disposition, and its palate may be purged and healthy, so that it may feel the rare and sublime touches of Divine love, wherein it will see itself divinely transformed, and all the contrarieties, whether actual or habitual, which it had aforetime, will be expelled, as we are saying.

4. Moreover, in order to attain the said union to which this dark night is disposing and leading it, the soul must be filled and endowed with a certain glorious magnificence in its communion with God, which includes within itself innumerable blessings springing from delights which exceed all the abundance that the soul can naturally possess. For by nature the soul is so weak and impure that it cannot receive all this. As Isaias says: "Eye hath not seen, nor ear heard, neither hath it entered into the heart of man, that which God hath prepared, etc."[4] It is meet, then, that the soul be first of all brought into emptiness and poverty of spirit and purged from all help, consolation and natural apprehension with respect to all things, both above and below. In this way, being empty, it is able indeed to be poor in spirit and freed from the old man, in order to live that new and blessed life which is attained by means of this night, and which is the state of union with God.

5. And because the soul is to attain to the possession of a sense, and of a Divine knowledge, which is very generous and full of sweetness, with respect to things Divine and human, which fall not within the common experience and natural knowledge of the soul (because it looks on them with eyes as different from those of the past as spirit is different from sense and the Divine from the human), the spirit must be straitened and inured to hardships as regards its common and natural experience, and be brought by means of this purgative contemplation into great anguish and affliction, and the memory must be borne far from all agreeable and peaceful knowledge, and have an intimate sense and feeling that it is making a pilgrimage and being a stranger to all things, so that it seems to it that all things are strange and of a different kind from that which they were wont to be. For this night is gradually drawing the spirit away from its ordinary and common experience of things and bringing it nearer the Divine sense, which is a stranger and an alien to all human ways. It seems now to the soul that it is going forth from its very self, with much affliction. At other times

---

[3] Tobias viii, 2.
[4] Isaias lxiv, 4 [1 Corinthians ii, 9].

it wonders if it is under a charm or a spell, and it goes about marvelling at the things that it sees and hears, which seem to it very strange and rare, though they are the same that it was accustomed to experience aforetime. The reason of this is that the soul is now becoming alien and remote from common sense and knowledge of things, in order that, being annihilated in this respect, it may be informed with the Divine — which belongs rather to the next life than to this.

6. The soul suffers all these afflictive purgations of the spirit to the end that it may be begotten anew in spiritual life by means of this Divine inflowing, and in these pangs may bring forth the spirit of salvation, that the saying of Isaias may be fulfilled: "In Thy sight, O Lord, we have conceived, and we have been as in the pangs of labor, and we have brought forth the spirit of salvation."[5] Moreover, since by means of this contemplative night the soul is prepared for the attainment of inward peace and tranquillity, which is of such a kind and so delectable that, as the Scripture says, it passes all understanding,[6] it behoves the soul to abandon all its former peace. This was in reality no peace at all, since it was involved in imperfections; but to the soul aforementioned it appeared to be so, because it was following its own inclinations, which were for peace. It seemed, indeed, to be a twofold peace — that is, the soul believed that it had already acquired the peace of sense and that of spirit, for it found itself to be full of the spiritual abundance of this peace of sense and of spirit — as I say, it is still imperfect. First of all, then, it must be purged of that former peace and disquieted concerning it and withdrawn from it. Even so was Jeremias when, in the passage which we quoted from him, he felt and lamented thus, in order to express the calamities of this night that is past, saying: "My soul is withdrawn and removed from peace."[7]

7. This is a painful disturbance, involving many misgivings, imaginings and strivings which the soul has within itself, wherein, with the apprehension and realization of the miseries in which it sees itself, it fancies that it is lost and that its blessings have gone for ever. Wherefore the spirit experiences pain and sighing so deep that they cause it vehement spiritual groans and cries, to which at times it gives vocal expression; when it has the necessary strength and power it dissolves into tears, although this relief comes but seldom. David describes this very aptly, in a Psalm, as one who has had experience of it, where he says: "I was exceedingly afflicted and humbled; I roared with the groaning of

---

[5] Isaias xxvi, 17–18.
[6] [Philippians iv, 7.]
[7] Lamentations iii, 17.

my heart."[8] This roaring implies great pain; for at times, with the sudden and acute remembrance of these miseries wherein the soul sees itself, pain and affliction rise up and surround it, and I know not how the affections of the soul could be described save in the similitude of holy Job, when he was in the same trials, and uttered these words: "Even as the overflowing of the waters, even so is my roaring."[9] For just as at times the waters make such inundations that they overwhelm and fill everything, so at times this roaring and this affliction of the soul grow to such an extent that they overwhelm it and penetrate it completely, filling it with spiritual pain and anguish in all its deep affections and energies, to an extent surpassing all possibility of exaggeration.

8. Such is the work wrought in the soul by this night that hides the hopes of the light of day. With regard to this the prophet Job says likewise: "In the night my mouth is pierced with sorrows and they that feed upon me sleep not."[10] Now here by the mouth is understood the will, which is transpierced with these pains that tear the soul to pieces, neither ceasing nor sleeping, for the doubts and misgivings which transpierce the soul in this way never cease.

9. Deep is this warfare and this striving, for the peace which the soul hopes for will be very deep; and the spiritual pain is intimate and delicate, for the love which it will possess will likewise be very intimate and refined. The more intimate and the more perfect the finished work is to be and to remain, the more intimate, perfect and pure must be the labor; the firmer the edifice, the harder the labor. Wherefore, as Job says, the soul is fading within itself, and its vitals are being consumed without any hope.[11] Similarly, because in the state of perfection toward which it journeys by means of this purgative night the soul will attain to the possession and fruition of innumerable blessings, of gifts and virtues, both according to the substance of the soul and likewise according to its faculties, it must needs see and feel itself withdrawn from them all and deprived of them all and be empty and poor without them; and it must needs believe itself to be so far from them that it cannot persuade itself that it will ever reach them, but rather it must be convinced that all its good things are over. The words of Jeremias have a similar meaning in that passage already quoted, where he says: "I have forgotten good things."[12]

10. But let us now see the reason why this light of contemplation,

---

[8] Psalm xxxviii, 8.
[9] Job iii, 24.
[10] Job xxx, 17.
[11] Job xxx, 16.
[12] Lamentations iii, 17.

which is so sweet and blessed to the soul that there is naught more desirable (for, as has been said above, it is the same wherewith the soul must be united and wherein it must find all the good things in the state of perfection that it desires), produces, when it assails the soul, these beginnings which are so painful and these effects which are so disagreeable, as we have here said.

11. This question is easy for us to answer, by explaining, as we have already done in part, that the cause of this is that, in contemplation and the Divine inflowing, there is naught that of itself can cause affliction, but that they rather cause great sweetness and delight, as we shall say hereafter. The cause is rather the weakness and imperfection from which the soul then suffers, and the dispositions which it has in itself and which make it unfit for the reception of them. Wherefore, when the said Divine light assails the soul, it must needs cause it to suffer after the manner aforesaid.

CHAPTER X

Explains this purgation fully by a comparison.

FOR THE greater clearness of what has been said, and of what has still to be said, it is well to observe at this point that this purgative and loving knowledge or Divine light whereof we here speak acts upon the soul which it is purging and preparing for perfect union with it in the same way as fire acts upon a log of wood in order to transform it into itself; for material fire, acting upon wood, first of all begins to dry it, by driving out its moisture and causing it to shed the water which it contains within itself. Then it begins to make it black, dark and unsightly, and even to give forth a bad odor, and, as it dries it little by little, it brings out and drives away all the dark and unsightly accidents which are contrary to the nature of fire. And, finally, it begins to kindle it externally and give it heat, and at last transforms it into itself and makes it as beautiful as fire. In this respect, the wood has neither passivity nor activity of its own, save for its weight, which is greater, and its substance, which is denser, than that of fire, for it has in itself the properties and activities of fire. Thus it is dry and it dries; it is hot and heats; it is bright and gives brightness; and it is much less heavy than before. All these properties and effects are caused in it by the fire.

2. In this same way we have to philosophize with respect to this Divine fire of contemplative love, which, before it unites and transforms the soul in itself, first purges it of all its contrary accidents. It

drives out its unsightliness, and makes it black and dark, so that it seems worse than before and more unsightly and abominable than it was wont to be. For this Divine purgation is removing all the evil and vicious humors which the soul has never perceived because they have been so deeply rooted and grounded in it; it has never realized, in fact, that it has had so much evil within itself. But now that they are to be driven forth and annihilated, these humors reveal themselves, and become visible to the soul because it is so brightly illumined by this dark light of Divine contemplation (although it is no worse than before, either in itself or in relation to God); and, as it sees in itself that which it saw not before, it is clear to it that not only is it unfit to be seen by God, but deserves His abhorrence, and that He does indeed abhor it. By this comparison we can now understand many things concerning what we are saying and purpose to say.

3. First, we can understand how the very light and the loving wisdom which are to be united with the soul and to transform it are the same that at the beginning purge and prepare it: even as the very fire which transforms the log of wood into itself, and makes it part of itself, is that which at the first was preparing it for that same purpose.

4. Secondly, we shall be able to see how these afflictions are not felt by the soul as coming from the said Wisdom, since, as the Wise Man says, all good things together come to the soul with her.[1] They are felt as coming from the weakness and imperfection which belong to the soul; without such purgation, the soul cannot receive its Divine light, sweetness and delight, even as the log of wood, when the fire acts upon it, cannot immediately be transformed until it be made ready; wherefore the soul is greatly afflicted. This statement is fully supported by the Preacher, where he describes all that he suffered in order that he might attain to union with wisdom and to the fruition of it, saying thus: "My soul hath wrestled with her and my bowels were moved in acquiring her; therefore it shall possess a good possession."[2]

5. Thirdly, we can learn here incidentally in what manner souls are afflicted in purgatory. For the fire would have no power over them, even though they came into contact with it, if they had no imperfections for which to suffer. These are the material upon which the fire of purgatory seizes; when that material is consumed there is naught else that can burn. So here, when the imperfections are consumed, the affliction of the soul ceases and its fruition remains.

6. The fourth thing that we shall learn here is the manner wherein the

---

[1] Wisdom vii, 11.
[2] Ecclesiasticus li, 19–21.

soul, as it becomes purged and purified by means of this fire of love, becomes ever more enkindled in love, just as the wood grows hotter in proportion as it becomes the better prepared by the fire. This enkindling of love, however, is not always felt by the soul, but only at times when contemplation assails it less vehemently, for then it has occasion to see, and even to enjoy, the work which is being wrought in it, and which is then revealed to it. For it seems that the worker takes his hand from the work, and draws the iron out of the furnace, in order that something of the work which is being done may be seen; and then there is occasion for the soul to observe in itself the good which it saw not while the work was going on. In the same way, when the flame ceases to attack the wood, it is possible to see how much of it has been enkindled.

7. Fifthly, we shall also learn from this comparison what has been said above — namely, how true it is that after each of these periods of relief the soul suffers once again, more intensely and keenly than before. For, after that revelation just referred to has been made, and after the more outward imperfections of the soul have been purified, the fire of love once again attacks that which has yet to be consumed and purified more inwardly. The suffering of the soul now becomes more intimate, subtle and spiritual, in proportion as the fire refines away the finer, more intimate and more spiritual imperfections, and those which are most deeply rooted in its inmost parts. And it is here just as with the wood, upon which the fire, when it begins to penetrate it more deeply, acts with more force and vehemence in preparing its most inward part to possess it.

8. Sixthly, we shall likewise learn here the reason why it seems to the soul that all its good is over, and that it is full of evil, since naught comes to it at this time but bitterness; it is like the burning wood, which is touched by no air nor by aught else than by consuming fire. But, when there occur other periods of relief like the first, the rejoicing of the soul will be more interior because the purification has been more interior also.

9. Seventhly, we shall learn that, although the soul has the most ample joy at these periods (so much so that, as we said, it sometimes thinks that its trials can never return again, although it is certain that they will return quickly), it cannot fail to realize, if it is aware (and at times it is made aware) of a root of imperfection which remains, that its joy is incomplete, because a new assault seems to be threatening it;[3] when this is so, the trial returns quickly. Finally, that which still remains to be purged and enlightened most inwardly cannot well be concealed from the soul in view of its experience of its former purification; even as also in the wood it is the

---

[3] [The sudden change of metaphor is the author's. The "assault" is, of course, the renewed growth of the "root."]

most inward part that remains longest unkindled, and the difference between it and that which has already been purged is clearly perceptible; and, when this purification once more assails it most inwardly, it is no wonder if it seems to the soul once more that all its good is gone, and that it never expects to experience it again, for, now that it has been plunged into these most inward sufferings, all good coming from without is over.

10. Keeping this comparison, then, before our eyes, together with what has already been said upon the first line of the first stanza concerning this dark night and its terrible properties, it will be well to leave these sad experiences of the soul and to begin to speak of the fruit of its tears and their blessed properties, whereof the soul begins to sing from this second line:

Kindled in love with yearnings.

CHAPTER XI

Begins to explain the second line of the first stanza. Describes how, as the fruit of these rigorous constraints, the soul finds itself with the vehement passion of Divine love.

IN THIS line the soul describes the fire of love which, as we have said, like the material fire acting upon the wood, begins to take hold upon the soul in this night of painful contemplation. This enkindling now described, although in a certain way it resembles that which we described above as coming to pass in the sensual part of the soul, is in some ways as different from that other as is the soul from the body, or the spiritual part from the sensual. For this present kind is an enkindling of spiritual love in the soul, which, in the midst of these dark confines, feels itself to be keenly and sharply wounded in strong Divine love, and to have a certain realization and foretaste of God, although it understands nothing definitely, for, as we say, the understanding is in darkness.

2. The spirit feels itself here to be deeply and passionately in love, for this spiritual enkindling produces the passion of love. And, inasmuch as this love is infused, it is passive rather than active, and thus it begets in the soul a strong passion of love. This love has in it something of union with God, and thus to some degree partakes of its properties, which are actions of God rather than of the soul, these being subdued within it passively. What the soul does here is to give its consent; the warmth and strength and temper and passion of love—or enkindling, as the soul here calls it—belong only to the love of God, which enters increasingly into

union with it. This love finds in the soul more occasion and preparation to unite itself with it and to wound it, according as all the soul's desires are the more recollected, and are the more withdrawn from and disabled for the enjoyment of aught either in Heaven or in earth.

3. This takes place to a great extent, as has already been said, in this dark purgation, for God has so weaned all the inclinations and caused them to be so recollected that they cannot find pleasure in anything they may wish. All this is done by God to the end that, when He withdraws them and recollects them in Himself, the soul may have more strength and fitness to receive this strong union of love of God, which He is now beginning to give it through this purgative way, wherein the soul must love with great strength and with all its desires and powers both of spirit and of sense; which could not be if they were dispersed in the enjoyment of aught else. For this reason David said to God, to the end that he might receive the strength of the love of this union with God: "I will keep my strength for Thee";[1] that is, I will keep the entire capacity and all the desires and energies of my faculties, nor will I employ their operation or pleasure in aught else than Thyself.

4. In this way it can be realized in some measure how great and how strong may be this enkindling of love in the spirit, wherein God keeps in recollection all the energies, faculties and desires of the soul, both of spirit and of sense, so that all this harmony may employ its energies and virtues in this love, and may thus attain to a true fulfilment of the first commandment, which sets aside nothing pertaining to man nor excludes from this love anything that is his, but says: "Thou shalt love thy God with all thy heart and with all thy mind, with all thy soul and with all thy strength."[2]

5. When all the desires and energies of the soul, then, have been recollected in this enkindling of love, and when the soul itself has been touched and wounded in them all, and has been inspired with passion, what shall we understand the movements and digressions of all these energies and desires to be, if they find themselves enkindled and wounded with strong love and without the possession and satisfaction thereof, in darkness and doubt? They will doubtless be suffering hunger, like the dogs of which David speaks as running about the city;[3] finding no satisfaction in this love, they keep howling and groaning. For the touch of this love and Divine fire dries up the spirit and enkindles its desires, in order to satisfy its thirst for this Divine love, so much so that it turns upon itself a thousand times and desires God in a thousand ways and manners, with the eagerness and

---

[1] Psalm lix, 9.
[2] Deuteronomy vi, 5.
[3] Psalm lix, 14–15.

desire of the appetite. This is very well explained by David in a psalm, where he says: "My soul thirsted for Thee: in how many manners does my soul long for Thee!"[4]—that is, in desires. And another version reads: "My soul thirsted for Thee, my soul is lost (*or* perishes) for Thee."

6. It is for this reason that the soul says in this line that it was "kindled in love with yearnings." For in all the things and thoughts that it revolves within itself, and in all the affairs and matters that present themselves to it, it loves in many ways, and also desires and suffers in the desire in many ways, at all times and in all places, finding rest in naught, and feeling this yearning in its enkindled wound, even as the prophet Job declares, saying: "As the hart[5] desireth the shadow, and as the hireling desireth the end of his work, so I also had vain months and numbered to myself wearisome and laborious nights. If I lie down to sleep, I shall say: 'When shall I arise?' And then I shall await the evening and shall be full of sorrows even until the darkness of night."[6] Everything becomes cramping to this soul: it cannot live within itself; it cannot live either in Heaven or on earth; and it is filled with griefs until the darkness comes to which Job here refers, speaking spiritually and in the sense of our interpretation. What the soul here endures is affliction and suffering without the consolation of a certain hope of any light and spiritual good. Wherefore the yearning and the grief of this soul in this enkindling of love are greater because it is multiplied in two ways: first, by the spiritual darkness wherein it finds itself, which afflicts it with its doubts and misgivings; and then by the love of God, which enkindles and stimulates it, and, with its loving wound, causes it a wondrous fear. These two kinds of suffering at such a season are well described by Isaias, where he says: "My soul desired Thee in the night"[7]—that is, in misery.

7. This is one kind of suffering which proceeds from this dark night; but, he goes on to say, with my spirit, in my bowels, until the morning, I will watch for Thee. And this is the second way of grieving in desire and yearning which comes from love in the bowels of the spirit, which are the spiritual affections. But in the midst of these dark and loving afflictions the soul feels within itself a certain companionship and strength, which bears it company and so greatly strengthens it that, if

---

[4] Psalm lxii, 1.
[5] [For *ciervo*, hart, read *siervo*, servant, and we have the correct quotation from Scripture. The change, however, was evidently made by the Saint knowingly. In P. Gerardo's edition, the Latin text, with *cervus*, precedes the Spanish translation, with *ciervo*.]
[6] Job vii, 2–4.
[7] Isaias xxvi, 9.

his burden of grievous darkness be taken away, it often feels itself to be
alone, empty and weak. The cause of this is that, as the strength and
efficacy of the soul were derived and communicated passively from the
dark fire of love which assailed it, it follows that, when that fire ceases
to assail it, the darkness and power and heat of love cease in the soul.

CHAPTER XII

*Shows how this horrible night is purgatory, and how in it the Divine wis-
dom illumines men on earth with the same illumination that purges and
illumines the angels in Heaven.*

FROM WHAT has been said we shall be able to see how this dark night
of loving fire, as it purges in the darkness, so also in the darkness enkindles the soul. We shall likewise be able to see that, even as spirits are
purged in the next life with dark material fire, so in this life they are
purged and cleansed with the dark spiritual fire of love. The difference
is that in the next life they are cleansed with fire, while here below they
are cleansed and illumined with love only. It was this love that David
entreated, when he said: *Cor mundum crea in me, Deus,* etc.[1] For
cleanness of heart is nothing less than the love and grace of God. For
the clean of heart are called by our Saviour "blessed"; which is as if He
had called them "enkindled with love," since blessedness is given by
nothing less than love.

2. And Jeremias well shows how the soul is purged when it is illumined with this fire of loving wisdom (for God never grants mystical
wisdom without love, since love itself infuses it), where he says: "He
hath sent fire into my bones, and hath taught me."[2] And David says that
the wisdom of God is silver tried in fire[3] — that is, in purgative fire of
love. For this dark contemplation infuses into the soul love and wisdom
jointly, to each one according to his capacity and need, enlightening
the soul and purging it, in the words of the Wise Man, from its ignorances, as he said was done to himself.

3. From this we shall also infer that the very wisdom of God which
purges these souls and illumines them purges the angels from their

---

[1] Psalm li, 10.
[2] Lamentations i, 13.
[3] Psalm xii, 6.

ignorances, giving them knowledge, enlightening them as to that which they knew not, and flowing down from God through the first hierarchies even to the last, and thence to men.[4] All the works, therefore, which are done by the angels, and all their inspirations, are said in the Scriptures, with truth and propriety, to be the work of God and of themselves; for ordinarily these inspirations come through the angels, and they receive them likewise one from another without any delay—as quickly as a ray of sunshine is communicated through many windows arranged in order. For although it is true that the sun's ray itself passes through them all, still each one passes it on and infuses it into the next, in a modified form, according to the nature of the glass, and with rather more or rather less power and brightness, according as it is nearer to the sun or farther from it.

4. Hence it follows that, the nearer to God are the higher spirits and the lower, the more completely are they purged and enlightened with more general purification; and that the lowest of them will receive this illumination very much less powerfully and more remotely. Hence it follows that man, who is the lowest of all those to whom this loving contemplation flows down continually from God, will, when God desires to give it him, receive it perforce after his own manner in a very limited way and with great pain. For, when the light of God illumines an angel, it enlightens him and enkindles him in love, since, being pure spirit, he is prepared for that infusion. But, when it illumines man, who is impure and weak, it illumines him, as has been said above, according to his nature. It plunges him into darkness and causes him affliction and distress, as does the sun to the eye that is weak; it enkindles him with passionate yet afflictive love, until he be spiritualized and refined by this same fire of love; and it purifies him until he can receive with sweetness the union of this loving infusion after the manner of the angels, being now purged, as by the help of the Lord we shall explain later. But meanwhile he receives this contemplation and loving knowledge in the constraint and yearning of love of which we are here speaking.

5. This enkindling and yearning of love are not always perceived by the soul. For in the beginning, when this spiritual purgation commences, all this Divine fire is used in drying up and making ready the wood (which is the soul) rather than in giving it heat. But, as time goes on, the fire begins

---

[4] The Schoolmen frequently assert that the lower angels are purged and illumined by the higher. Cf. St. Thomas, *Summa*, I, q. 106, a. 1, ad. 1.

o give heat to the soul, and the soul then very commonly feels this enkindling and heat of love. Further, as the understanding is being more and more purged by means of this darkness, it sometimes comes to pass that this mystical and loving theology, as well as enkindling the will, strikes and illumines the other faculty also—that of the understanding—with a certain Divine light and knowledge, so delectably and delicately that it aids the will to conceive a marvellous fervour, and, without any action of its own, there burns in it this Divine fire of love, in living flames, so that it now appears to the soul a living fire by reason of the living understanding which is given to it. It is of this that David speaks in a Psalm, saying: "My heart grew hot within me, and, as I meditated, a certain fire was enkindled."[5]

6. This enkindling of love, which accompanies the union of these two faculties, the understanding and the will, which are here united, is for the soul a thing of great richness and delight; for it is a certain touch of the Divinity and is already the beginning of the perfection of the union of love for which it hopes. Now the soul attains not to this touch of so sublime a sense and love of God, save when it has passed through many trials and a great part of its purgation. But for other touches which are much lower than these, and which are of ordinary occurrence, so much purgation is not needful.

7. From what we have said it may here be inferred how in these spiritual blessings, which are passively infused by God into the soul, the will may very well love even though the understanding understand not; and similarly the understanding may understand and the will love not. For, since this dark night of contemplation consists of Divine light and love, just as fire contains light and heat, it is not unbefitting that, when this loving light is communicated, it should strike the will at times more effectively by enkindling it with love and leaving the understanding in darkness instead of striking it with light; and, at other times, by enlightening it with light, and giving it understanding, but leaving the will in aridity (as it is also true that the heat of the fire can be received without the light being seen, and also the light of it can be seen without the reception of heat); and this is wrought by the Lord, Who infuses as He wills.[6]

---

[5] Psalm xxxix, 3.

[6] The Saint here treats a question ofen debated by philosophers and mystics—that of love and knowldge. Cf. also *Spiritual Canticle*, Stanza XVII, and *Living Flame*, Stanza III. Philosophers generally maintain that it is impossible to love without knowledge, and equally so to love more of an object than what is known of it. Mystics have, however, their own solutions of the philosophers' difficulty and the speculative Spanish mystics have much to say on the matter. (Cf., for example, the *Médula Mística*, Trat. V, Chap. iv, and the *Escuela de Oración*, Trat. XII, Duda v.)

CHAPTER XIII

Of other delectable effects which are wrought in the soul by this dark night of contemplation.

THIS TYPE of enkindling will explain to us certain of the delectable effects which this dark night of contemplation works in the soul. For at certain times, as we have just said, the soul becomes enlightened in the midst of all this darkness, and the light shines in the darkness;[1] this mystical intelligence flows down into the understanding and the will remains in dryness—I mean, without actual union of love, with a serenity and simplicity which are so delicate and delectable to the sense of the soul that no name can be given to them. Thus the presence of God is felt, now after one manner, now after another.

2. Sometimes, too, as has been said, it wounds the will at the same time, and enkindles love sublimely, tenderly and strongly; for we have already said that at certain times these two faculties, the understanding and the will, are united, when, the more they see, the more perfect and delicate is the purgation of the understanding. But, before this state is reached, it is more usual for the touch of the enkindling of love to be felt in the will than for the touch of intelligence to be felt in the understanding.

3. But one question arises here, which is this: Why, since these two faculties are being purged together, are the enkindling and the love of purgative contemplation at first more commonly felt in the will than the intelligence thereof is felt in the understanding? To this it may be answered that this passive love does not now directly strike the will, for the will is free, and this enkindling of love is a passion of love rather than the free act of the will; for this heat of love strikes the substance of the soul and thus moves the affections passively. And so this is called passion of love rather than a free act of the will, an act of the will being so called only in so far as it is free. But these passions and affections subdue the will, and therefore it is said that, if the soul conceives passion with a certain affection, the will conceives passion; and this is indeed so, for in this manner the will is taken captive and loses its liberty, according as the impetus and power of its passion carry it away. And therefore we can say that this enkindling of love is in the will—that is, it enkindles the desire of the will; and thus, as we say, this is called passion of love rather than the free work of the will. And, because the receptive passion of the understanding can receive intelligence

---

[1] St. John i, 5.

only in a detached and passive way (and this is impossible without its having been purged), therefore until this happens the soul feels the touch of intelligence less frequently than that of the passion of love. For it is not necessary to this end that the will should be so completely purged with respect to the passions, since these very passions help it to feel impassioned love.

4. This enkindling and thirst of love, which in this case belongs to the spirit, is very different from that other which we described in writing of the night of sense. For, though the sense has also its part here, since it fails not to participate in the labor of the spirit, yet the source and the keenness of the thirst of love is felt in the superior part of the soul—that is, in the spirit. It feels, and understands what it feels and its lack of what it desires, in such a way that all its affliction of sense, although greater without comparison than in the first night of sense, is as naught to it, because it recognizes within itself the lack of a great good which can in no way be measured.

5. But here we must note that although, at the beginning, when this spiritual night commences, this enkindling of love is not felt, because this fire of love has not begun to take a hold, God gives the soul, in place of it, an estimative love of Himself so great that, as we have said, the greatest sufferings and trials of which it is conscious in this night are the anguished thoughts that it has lost God and the fears that He has abandoned it. And thus we may always say that from the very beginning of this night the soul is touched with yearnings of love, which is now that of estimation,[2] and now again, that of enkindling. And it is evident that the greatest suffering which it feels in these trials is this misgiving; for, if it could be certified at that time that all is not lost and over, but that what is happening to it is for the best—as it is—and that God is not wroth, it would care naught for all these afflictions, but would rejoice to know that God is making use of them for His good pleasure. For the love of estimation which it has for God is so great, even though it may not realize this and may be in darkness, that it would be glad, not only to suffer in this way, but even to die many times over in order to give Him satisfaction. But when once the flame has enkindled the soul, it is wont to conceive, together with the estimation that it already has for God, such power and energy, and such yearning for Him, when He communicates to it the heat of love, that, with great boldness, it disregards every-

---

[2] [The word translated "estimation" might also be rendered "reverent love." The "love of estimation," which has its seat in the understanding, is contrasted with the "enkindling" or the "love of desire," which has its seat in the will. So elsewhere in this paragraph.]

thing and ceases to pay respect to anything, such are the power and the inebriation of love and desire. It regards not what it does, for it would do strange and unusual things in whatever way and manner may present themselves, if thereby its soul might find Him Whom it loves.

6. It was for this reason that Mary Magdalene, though as greatly concerned for her own appearance as she was aforetime, took no heed of the multitude of men who were at the feast, whether they were of little or of great importance; neither did she consider that it was not seemly, and that it looked ill, to go and weep and shed tears among the guests, provided that, without delaying an hour or waiting for another time and season, she could reach Him for love of Whom her soul was already wounded and enkindled. And such is the inebriating power and the boldness of love, that, though she knew her Beloved to be enclosed in the sepulchre by the great sealed stone, and surrounded by soldiers who were guarding Him lest His disciples should steal Him away,[3] she allowed none of these things to impede her, but went before daybreak with the ointments to anoint Him.

7. And finally, this inebriating power and yearning of love caused her to ask one whom she believed to be a gardener and to have stolen Him away from the sepulchre, to tell her, if he had taken Him, where he had laid Him, that she might take Him away;[4] considering not that such a question, according to independent judgment and reason, was foolish; for it was evident that, if the other had stolen Him, he would not say so, still less would he allow Him to be taken away. It is a characteristic of the power and vehemence of love that all things seem possible to it, and it believes all men to be of the same mind as itself. For it thinks that there is naught wherein one may be employed, or which one may seek, save that which it seeks itself and that which it loves; and it believes that there is naught else to be desired, and naught wherein it may be employed, save that one thing, which is pursued by all. For this reason, when the Bride went out to seek her Beloved, through streets and squares, thinking that all others were doing the same, she begged them that, if they found Him, they would speak to Him and say that she was pining for love of Him.[5] Such was the power of the love of this Mary that she thought that,

---

[3] St. John xx, 1 [St. Matthew xxvii, 62–66].
[4] St. John xx, 15.
[5] Canticles v, 8.

if the gardener would tell her where he had hidden Him, she would go and take Him away, however difficult it might be made for her.

8. Of this manner, then, are the yearnings of love whereof this soul becomes conscious when it has made some progress in this spiritual purgation. For it rises up by night (that is, in this purgative darkness) according to the affections of the will. And with the yearnings and vehemence of the lioness or the she-bear going to seek her cubs when they have been taken away from her and she finds them not, does this wounded soul go forth to seek its God. For, being in darkness, it feels itself to be without Him and to be dying of love for Him. And this is that impatient love wherein the soul cannot long subsist without gaining its desire or dying. Such was Rachel's desire for children when she said to Jacob: "Give me children, else shall I die."[6]

9. But we have now to see how it is that the soul which feels itself so miserable and so unworthy of God, here in this purgative darkness, has nevertheless strength, and is sufficiently bold and daring, to journey towards union with God. The reason is that, as love continually gives it strength wherewith it may love indeed, and as the property of love is to desire to be united, joined and made equal and like to the object of its love, that it may perfect itself in love's good things, hence it comes to pass that, when this soul is not perfected in love, through not having as yet attained to union, the hunger and thirst that it has for that which it lacks (which is union) and the strength set by love in the will which has caused it to become impassioned, make it bold and daring by reason of the enkindling of its will, although in its understanding, which is still dark and unenlightened, it feels itself to be unworthy and knows itself to be miserable.

10. I will not here omit to mention the reason why this Divine light, which is always light to the soul, illumines it not as soon as it strikes it, as it does afterwards, but causes it the darkness and the trials of which we have spoken. Something has already been said concerning this, but the question must now be answered directly. The darkness and the other evils of which the soul is conscious when this Divine light strikes it are not darkness or evils caused by this light, but pertain to the soul itself, and the light illumines it so that it may see them. Wherefore it does indeed receive light from this Divine light; but the soul cannot see at first, by its aid, anything beyond what is nearest to it, or rather, beyond what is

---

[6] Genesis xxxi, 1.

within it—namely, its darknesses or its miseries, which it now sees
through the mercy of God, and saw not aforetime, because this supernatural light illumined it not. And this is the reason why at first it is conscious of nothing beyond darkness and evil; after it has been purged,
however, by means of the knowledge and realization of these, it will
have eyes to see, by the guidance of this light, the blessings of the
Divine light; and, once all these darknesses and imperfections have
been driven out from the soul, it seems that the benefits and the great
blessings which the soul is gaining in this blessed night of contemplation become clearer.

11. From what has been said, it is clear that God grants the soul in
this state the favor of purging it and healing it with this strong lye of bitter purgation, according to its spiritual and its sensual part, of all the
imperfect habits and affections which it had within itself with respect
to temporal things and to natural, sensual and spiritual things, its
inward faculties being darkened, and voided of all these, its spiritual
and sensual affections being constrained and dried up, and its natural
energies being attenuated and weakened with respect to all this (a condition which it could never attain of itself, as we shall shortly say). In
this way God makes it to die to all that is not naturally God, so that,
once it is stripped and denuded of its former skin, He may begin to
clothe it anew. And thus its youth is renewed like the eagle's and it is
clothed with the new man, which, as the Apostle says, is created
according to God.[7] This is naught else but His illumination of the
understanding with supernatural light, so that it is no more a human
understanding but becomes Divine through union with the Divine. In
the same way the will is informed with Divine love, so that it is a will
that is now no less than Divine, nor does it love otherwise than divinely,
for it is made and united in one with the Divine will and love. So, too,
is it with the memory; and likewise the affections and desires are all
changed and converted divinely, according to God. And thus this soul
will now be a soul of heaven, heavenly, and more Divine than human.
All this, as we have been saying, and because of what we have said, God
continues to do and to work in the soul by means of this night, illumining and enkindling it divinely with yearnings for God alone and for
naught else whatsoever. For which cause the soul then very justly and
reasonably adds the third line to the song, which says:

> . . . oh, happy chance!—
> **I went forth without being observed.**

---

[7] Ephesians iv, 24.

CHAPTER XIV

Wherein are set down and explained the last three lines of the first stanza.

THIS HAPPY chance was the reason for which the soul speaks, in the next lines, as follows:

I went forth without being observed,   My house being now at rest.

It takes the metaphor from one who, in order the better to accomplish something, leaves his house by night and in the dark, when those that are in the house are now at rest, so that none may hinder him. For this soul had to go forth to perform a deed so heroic and so rare—namely to become united with its Divine Beloved—and it had to leave its house, because the Beloved is not found save alone and without, in solitude. It was for this reason that the Bride desired to find Him alone, saying: "Who would give Thee to me, my brother, that I might find Thee alone, without, and that my love might be communicated to Thee."[1] It is needful for the enamoured soul, in order to attain to its desired end, to do likewise, going forth at night, when all the domestics in its house are sleeping and at rest—that is, when the low operations, passions and desires of the soul (who are the people of the household) are, because it is night, sleeping and at rest. When these are awake, they invariably hinder the soul from seeking its good, since they are opposed to its going forth in freedom. These are they of whom Our Saviour speaks in the Gospel, saying that they are the enemies of man.[2] And thus it would be meet that their operations and motions should be put to sleep in this night, to the end that they may not hinder the soul from attaining the supernatural blessings of the union of love of God, for, while these are alive and active, this cannot be. For all their work and their natural motions hinder, rather than aid, the soul's reception of the spiritual blessings of the union of love, inasmuch as all natural ability is impotent with respect to the supernatural blessings that God, by means of His own infusion, bestows upon the soul passively, secretly and in silence. And thus it is needful that all the faculties should receive this infusion, and that, in order to receive it, they should remain passive, and not interpose their own base acts and vile inclinations.

---

[1] Canticles viii, 1.
[2] St. Matthew x, 36.

2. It was a happy chance for this soul that on this night God should put to sleep all the domestics in its house—that is, all the faculties, passions, affections and desires which live in the soul, both sensually and spiritually. For thus it went forth "without being observed"—that is, without being hindered by these affections, etc., for they were put to sleep and mortified in this night, in the darkness of which they were left, that they might not notice or feel anything after their own low and natural manner, and might thus be unable to hinder the soul from going forth from itself and from the house of its sensuality. And thus only could the soul attain to the spiritual union of perfect love of God.

3. Oh, how happy a chance is this for the soul which can free itself from the house of its sensuality! None can understand it, unless, as it seems to me, it be the soul that has experienced it. For such a soul will see clearly how wretched was the servitude in which it lay and to how many miseries it was subject when it was at the mercy of its faculties and desires, and will know how the life of the spirit is true liberty and wealth, bringing with it inestimable blessings. Some of these we shall point out, as we proceed, in the following stanzas, wherein it will be seen more clearly what good reason the soul has to sing of the happy chance of its passage from this dreadful night which has been described above.

CHAPTER XV

Sets down the second stanza and its exposition.

In darkness and secure,　By the secret ladder, disguised—oh, happy
　　chance!
In darkness and concealment,　My house being now at rest.

IN THIS stanza the soul still continues to sing of certain properties of the darkness of this night, reiterating how great is the happiness which came to it through them. It speaks of them in replying to a certain tacit objection, saying that it is not to be supposed that, because in this night and darkness it has passed through so many tempests of afflictions, doubts, fears and horrors, as has been said, it has for that reason run any risk of being lost. On the contrary, it says, in the darkness of this night it has gained itself. For in the night it has freed itself and escaped subtly from its enemies, who were continually hindering its progress. For in the darkness of the night it changed its garments and disguised itself with three liveries and colors which we shall describe hereafter; and went forth by a very secret ladder, which none in the house knew, the which ladder, as we shall observe likewise in the proper place, is living faith. By this ladder the soul went forth in such complete hiding and concealment, in order the better to execute its purpose, that it could not fail to be in great security; above all since in this purgative night the desires, affections and passions of the soul are put to sleep, mortified and quenched, which are they that, when they were awake and alive, consented not to this.

The first line, then, runs thus:

In darkness and secure.

CHAPTER XVI

Explains how, though in darkness, the soul walks securely.

THE DARKNESS which the soul here describes relates, as we have said, to the desires and faculties, sensual, interior and spiritual, for all these are darkened in this night as to their natural light, so that, being purged in this respect, they may be illumined with respect to the supernatural. For the spiritual and the sensual desires are put to sleep and mortified, so that they can experience nothing, either Divine or human; the affections of the soul are oppressed and constrained, so that they can neither move nor find support in anything; the imagination is bound and can make no useful reflection; the memory is gone; the understanding is in darkness, unable to understand anything; and hence the will likewise is arid and constrained and all the faculties are void and useless; and in addition to all this a thick and heavy cloud is upon the soul, keeping it in affliction, and, as it were, far away from God.[1] It is in this kind of "darkness" that the soul says here it travelled "securely."

2. The reason for this has been clearly expounded; for ordinarily the soul never strays save through its desires or its tastes or its reflections or its

---

[1] Some have considered this description exaggerated, but it must be borne in mind that all souls are not tested alike and the Saint is writing of those whom God has willed to raise to such sanctity that they drain the cup of bitterness to the dregs. We have already seen (Bk. I, chap. XIV, section 5) that "all do not experience (this) after one manner . . . for (it) is meted out by the will of God, in conformity with the greater or the smaller degree of imperfection which each soul has to purge away, (and) in conformity, likewise, with the degree of love of union to which God is pleased to raise it."

understanding or its affections; for as a rule it has too much or too little of these, or they vary or go astray, and hence the soul becomes inclined to that which behoves it not. Wherefore, when all these operations and motions are hindered, it is clear that the soul is secure against being led astray by them; for it is free, not only from itself, but likewise from its other enemies, which are the world and the devil. For when the affections and operations of the soul are quenched, these enemies cannot make war upon it by any other means or in any other manner.

3. It follows from this that, the greater is the darkness wherein the soul journeys and the more completely is it voided of its natural operations, the greater is its security. For, as the Prophet says,[2] perdition comes to the soul from itself alone—that is, from its sensual and interior desires and operations; and good, says God, comes from Me alone. Wherefore, when it is thus hindered from following the things that lead it into evil, there will then come to it forthwith the blessings of union with God in its desires and faculties, which in that union He will make Divine and celestial. Hence, at the time of this darkness, if the soul considers the matter, it will see very clearly how little its desire and its faculties are being diverted to things that are useless and harmful; and how secure it is from vainglory and pride and presumption, vain and false rejoicing and many other things. It follows clearly, then, that, by walking in darkness, not only is the soul not lost, but it has even greatly gained, since it is here gaining the virtues.

4. But there is a question which at once arises here—namely, since the things of God are of themselves profitable to the soul and bring it gain and security, why does God, in this night, darken the desires and faculties with respect to these good things likewise, in such a way that the soul can no more taste of them or busy itself with them than with these other things, and indeed in some ways can do so less? The answer is that it is well for the soul to perform no operation touching spiritual things at that time and to have no pleasure in such things, because its faculties and desires are base, impure and wholly natural; and thus, although these faculties be given the desire and interest in things supernatural and Divine, they could not receive them save after a base and a natural manner, exactly in their own fashion. For, as the philosopher says, whatsoever is received comes to him that receives it after the manner of the recipient. Wherefore, since these natural faculties have neither purity nor strength nor capacity to receive and taste things that are supernatural after the

---

[2] Osee xiii, 9.

manner of those things, which manner is Divine, but can do so only after their own manner, which is human and base, as we have said, it is meet that its faculties be in darkness concerning these Divine things likewise. Thus, being weaned and purged and annihilated in this respect first of all, they may lose that base and human way of receiving and acting, and thus all these faculties and desires of the soul may come to be prepared and tempered in such a way as to be able to receive, feel and taste that which is Divine and supernatural after a sublime and lofty manner, which is impossible if the old man die not first of all.

5. Hence it follows that all spiritual things, if they come not from above and be not communicated by the Father of lights to human desire and free will (howsoever much a man may exercise his taste and faculties for God, and howsoever much it may seem to the faculties that they are experiencing these things), will not be experienced after a Divine and spiritual manner, but after a human and natural manner, just as other things are experienced, for spiritual blessings go not from man to God, but come from God to man. With respect to this (if this were the proper place for it) we might here explain how there are many persons whose many tastes and affections and the operations of whose faculties are fixed upon God or upon spiritual things, and who may perhaps think that this is supernatural and spiritual, when it is perhaps no more than the most human and natural desires and actions. They regard these good things with the same disposition as they have for other things, by means of a certain natural facility which they possess for directing their desires and faculties to anything whatever.

6. If perchance we find occasion elsewhere in this book, we shall treat of this, describing certain signs which indicate when the interior actions and motions of the soul, with respect to communion with God, are only natural, when they are spiritual, and when they are both natural and spiritual. It suffices for us here to know that, in order that the interior motions and acts of the soul may come to be moved by God divinely, they must first be darkened and put to sleep and hushed to rest naturally as touching all their capacity and operation, until they have no more strength.

7. Therefore, O spiritual soul, when thou seest thy desire obscured, thy affections arid and constrained, and thy faculties bereft of their capacity for any interior exercise, be not afflicted by this, but rather consider it a great happiness, since God is freeing thee from thyself and taking the matter from thy hands. For with those hands, howsoever well they may serve thee, thou wouldst never labor so effectively, so perfectly and so securely (because of their clumsiness and uncleanness) as now, when God takes thy hand and guides thee in the darkness, as

though thou wert blind, to an end and by a way which thou knowest not. Nor couldst thou ever hope to travel with the aid of thine own eyes and feet, howsoever good thou be as a walker.

8. The reason, again, why the soul not only travels securely, when it travels thus in the darkness, but also achieves even greater gain and progress, is that usually, when the soul is receiving fresh advantage and profit, this comes by a way that it least understands—indeed, it quite commonly believes that it is losing ground. For, as it has never experienced that new feeling which drives it forth and dazzles it and makes it depart recklessly from its former way of life, it thinks itself to be losing ground rather than gaining and progressing, since it sees that it is losing with respect to that which it knew and enjoyed, and is going by a way which it knows not and wherein it finds no enjoyment. It is like the traveller, who, in order to go to new and unknown lands, takes new roads, unknown and untried, and journeys unguided by his past experience, but doubtingly and according to what others say. It is clear that such a man could not reach new countries, or add to his past experience, if he went not along new and unknown roads and abandoned those which were known to him. Exactly so, one who is learning fresh details concerning any office or art always proceeds in darkness, and receives no guidance from his original knowledge, for if he left not that behind he would get no farther nor make any progress; and in the same way, when the soul is making most progress, it is travelling in darkness, knowing naught. Wherefore, since God, as we have said, is the Master and Guide of this blind soul, it may well and truly rejoice, once it has learned to understand this, and say: "In darkness and secure."

9. There is another reason why the soul has walked securely in this darkness, and this is because it has been suffering; for the road of suffering is more secure and even more profitable than that of fruition and action: first, because in suffering the strength of God is added to that of man, while in action and fruition the soul is practicing its own weaknesses and imperfections; and second, because in suffering the soul continues to practice and acquire the virtues and become purer, wiser and more cautious.

10. But there is another and a more important reason why the soul now walks in darkness and securely; this emanates from the dark light or wisdom aforementioned. For in such a way does this dark night of contemplation absorb and immerse the soul in itself, and so near does it bring the soul to God, that it protects and delivers it from all that is not God. For this soul is now, as it were, undergoing a cure, in order that it may regain its health—its health being God Himself. His Majesty restricts it to a diet and abstinence from all things, and takes away its appetite for them all. It is like a sick man, who, if he is

respected by those in his house, is carefully tended so that he may be cured; the air is not allowed to touch him, nor may he even enjoy the light, nor must he hear footsteps, nor yet the noise of those in the house; and he is given food that is very delicate, and even that only in great moderation—food that is nourishing rather than delectable.

11. All these particularities (which are for the security and safekeeping of the soul) are caused by this dark contemplation, because it brings the soul nearer to God. For the nearer the soul approaches Him, the blacker is the darkness which it feels and the deeper is the obscurity which comes through its weakness; just as, the nearer a man approaches the sun, the greater are the darkness and the affliction caused him through the great splendour of the sun and through the weakness and impurity of his eyes. In the same way, so immense is the spiritual light of God, and so greatly does it transcend our natural understanding, that the nearer we approach it, the more it blinds and darkens us. And this is the reason why, in Psalm xvii, David says that God made darkness His hiding-place and covering, and His tabernacle around Him dark water in the clouds of the air.[3] This dark water in the clouds of the air is dark contemplation and Divine wisdom in souls, as we are saying. They continue to feel it as a thing which is near Him, as the tabernacle wherein He dwells, when God brings them ever nearer to Himself. And thus, that which in God is supreme light and refulgence is to man blackest darkness, as Saint Paul says, according as David explains in the same Psalm, saying: "Because of the brightness which is in His presence, passed clouds and cataracts"[4]—that is to say, over the natural understanding, the light whereof, as Isaias says in Chapter V: *Obtenebrata est in caligine ejus.*[5]

12. Oh, miserable is the fortune of our life, which is lived in such great peril and wherein it is so difficult to find the truth! For that which is most clear and true is to us most dark and doubtful; wherefore, though it is the thing that is most needful for us, we flee from it. And that which gives the greatest light and satisfaction to our eyes we embrace and pursue, though it be the worst thing for us, and make us fall at every step. In what peril and fear does man live, since the very natural light of his eyes by which he has to guide himself is the first light that dazzles him and leads him astray on his road to God! And if he is to know with certainty by what road he travels, he must perforce keep his eyes closed and walk in dark-

---

[3] Psalm xviii, 11.
[4] Psalm xviii, 12.
[5] Isaias v, 30.

ness, that he may be secure from the enemies who inhabit his own house—that is, his senses and faculties.

13. Well hidden, then, and well protected is the soul in these dark waters, when it is close to God. For, as these waters serve as a tabernacle and dwelling-place for God Himself, they will serve the soul in the same way and for a perfect protection and security, though it remain in darkness, wherein, as we have said, it is hidden and protected from itself, and from all evils that come from creatures; for to such the words of David refer in another Psalm, where he says: "Thou shalt hide them in the hiding-place of Thy face from the disturbance of men; Thou shalt protect them in Thy tabernacle from the contradiction of tongues."[6] Herein we understand all kinds of protection; for to be hidden in the face of God from the disturbance of men is to be fortified with this dark contemplation against all the chances which may come upon the soul from men. And to be protected in His tabernacle from the contradiction of tongues is for the soul to be engulfed in these dark waters, which are the tabernacle of David whereof we have spoken. Wherefore, since the soul has all its desires and affections weaned and its faculties set in darkness, it is free from all imperfections which contradict the spirit, whether they come from its own flesh or from other creatures. Wherefore this soul may well say that it journeys "in darkness and secure."

14. There is likewise another reason, which is no less effectual than the last, by which we may understand how the soul journeys securely in darkness; it is derived from the fortitude by which the soul is at once inspired in these obscure and afflictive dark waters of God. For after all, though the waters be dark, they are none the less waters, and therefore they cannot but refresh and fortify the soul in that which is most needful for it, although in darkness and with affliction. For the soul immediately perceives in itself a genuine determination and an effectual desire to do naught which it understands to be an offence to God, and to omit to do naught that seems to be for His service. For that dark love cleaves to the soul, causing it a most watchful care and an inward solicitude concerning that which it must do, or must not do, for His sake, in order to please Him. It will consider and ask itself a thousand times if it has given Him cause to be offended; and all this it will do with much greater care and solicitude than before, as has already been said with respect to the yearnings of love. For here all the desires and energies and faculties of the soul are recollected from all things else, and its

---

[6] Psalm xxxi, 20.

effort and strength are employed in pleasing its God alone. After this manner the soul goes forth from itself and from all created things to the sweet and delectable union of love of God, "In darkness and secure."

By the secret ladder, disguised.

CHAPTER XVII

Explains how this dark contemplation is secret.

THREE THINGS have to be expounded with reference to three words contained in this present line. Two (namely, "secret" and "ladder") belong to the dark night of contemplation of which we are treating; the third (namely, "disguised") belongs to the soul by reason of the manner wherein it conducts itself in this night. As to the first, it must be known that in this line the soul describes this dark contemplation, by which it goes forth to the union of love, as a secret ladder, because of the two properties which belong to it—namely, its being secret and its being a ladder. We shall treat of each separately.

2. First, it describes this dark contemplation as "secret," since, as we have indicated above, it is mystical theology, which theologians call secret wisdom, and which, as Saint Thomas says, is communicated and infused into the soul through love. This happens secretly and in darkness, so as to be hidden from the work of the understanding and of other faculties. Wherefore, inasmuch as the faculties aforementioned attain not to it, but the Holy Spirit infuses and orders it in the soul, as says the Bride in the Songs, without either its knowledge or its understanding, it is called secret. And, in truth, not only does the soul not understand it, but there is none that does so, not even the devil; inasmuch as the Master Who teaches the soul is within it in its substance, to which the devil may not attain, neither may natural sense nor understanding.

3. And it is not for this reason alone that it may be called secret, but likewise because of the effects which it produces in the soul. For it is secret not only in the darknesses and afflictions of purgation, when this wisdom of love purges the soul, and the soul is unable to speak of it, but equally so afterwards in illumination, when this wisdom is communicated to it most clearly. Even then it is still so secret that the soul cannot speak of it and give it a name whereby it may be called; for, apart from the fact that the soul has no desire to speak of it, it can find no suitable way or manner or similitude by which it may be able to

describe such lofty understanding and such delicate spiritual feeling. And thus, even though the soul might have a great desire to express it and might find many ways in which to describe it, it would still be secret and remain undescribed. For, as that inward wisdom is so simple, so general and so spiritual that it has not entered into the understanding enwrapped or cloaked in any form or image subject to sense, it follows that sense and imagination (as it has not entered through them nor has taken their form and color) cannot account for it or imagine it, so as to say anything concerning it, although the soul be clearly aware that it is experiencing and partaking of that rare and delectable wisdom. It is like one who sees something never seen before, whereof he has not even seen the like; although he might understand its nature and have experience of it, he would be unable to give it a name, or say what it is, however much he tried to do so, and this in spite of its being a thing which he had perceived with the senses. How much less, then, could he describe a thing that has not entered through the senses! For the language of God has this characteristic that, since it is very intimate and spiritual in its relations with the soul, it transcends every sense and at once makes all harmony and capacity of the outward and inward senses to cease and be dumb.

4. For this we have both authorities and examples in the Divine Scripture. For the incapacity of man to speak of it and describe it in words was shown by Jeremias,[1] when, after God had spoken with him, he knew not what to say, save "Ah, ah, ah!" This interior incapacity—that is, of the interior sense of the imagination—and also that of the exterior sense corresponding to it was also demonstrated in the case of Moses, when he stood before God in the bush;[2] not only did he say to God that after speaking with Him he knew not neither was able to speak, but also that not even (as is said in the Acts of the Apostles)[3] with the interior imagination did he dare to meditate, for it seemed to him that his imagination was very far away and was too dumb, not only to express any part of that which he understood concerning God, but even to have the capacity to receive aught therefrom. Wherefore, inasmuch as the wisdom of this contemplation is the language of God to the soul, addressed by pure spirit to pure spirit, naught that is less than spirit, such as the senses, can perceive it, and thus to them it is secret, and they know it not, neither can they say it, nor do they desire to do so, because they see it not.

5. We may deduce from this the reason why certain persons—good and fearful souls—who walk along this road and would like to give an

---

[1] Jeremias i, 6.
[2] Exodus iv, 10 [cf. iii, 2].
[3] Acts vii, 32.

account of their spiritual state to their director, are neither able to do so nor know how. For the reason we have described, they have a great repugnance in speaking of it, especially when their contemplation is of the purer sort, so that the soul itself is hardly conscious of it. Such a person is only able to say that he is satisfied, tranquil and contented and that he is conscious of the presence of God, and that, as it seems to him, all is going well with him; but he cannot describe the state of his soul, nor can he say anything about it save in general terms like these. It is a different matter when the experiences of the soul are of a particular kind, such as visions, feelings, etc., which, being ordinarily received under some species wherein sense participates, can be described under that species, or by some other similitude. But this capacity for being described is not in the nature of pure contemplation, which is indescribable, as we have said, for the which reason it is called secret.

6. And not only for that reason is it called secret, and is so, but likewise because this mystical knowledge has the property of hiding the soul within itself. For, besides performing its ordinary function, it sometimes absorbs the soul and engulfs it in its secret abyss, in such a way that the soul clearly sees that it has been carried far away from every creature and has become most remote therefrom; so that it considers itself as having been placed in a most profound and vast retreat, to which no human creature can attain, such as an immense desert, which nowhere has any boundary, a desert the more delectable, pleasant and lovely for its secrecy, vastness and solitude, wherein, the more the soul is raised up above all temporal creatures, the more deeply does it find itself hidden. And so greatly does this abyss of wisdom raise up and exalt the soul at this time, making it to penetrate the veins of the science of love, that it not only shows it how base are all properties of the creatures by comparison with this supreme knowledge and Divine feeling, but likewise it learns how base and defective, and, in some measure, how inapt, are all the terms and words which are used in this life to treat of Divine things, and how impossible it is, in any natural way or manner, however learnedly and sublimely they may be spoken of, to be able to know and perceive them as they are, save by the illumination of this mystical theology. And thus, when by means of this illumination the soul discerns this truth, namely, that it cannot reach it, still less explain it, by common or human language, it rightly calls it secret.

7. This property of secrecy and superiority over natural capacity, which belongs to this Divine contemplation, belongs to it, not only because it is supernatural, but also inasmuch as it is a road that guides and leads the soul to the perfections of union with God; which, as they are things unknown after a human manner, must be approached, after a human manner, by unknowing and by Divine ignorance. For, speaking mysti-

cally, as we are speaking here, Divine things and perfections are known and understood as they are, not when they are being sought after and practiced, but when they have been found and practiced. To this purpose speaks the prophet Baruch concerning this Divine wisdom: "There is none that can know her ways nor that can imagine her paths."[4] Likewise the royal Prophet speaks in this manner concerning this road of the soul, when he says to God: "Thy lightnings lighted and illumined the round earth; the earth was moved and trembled. Thy way is in the sea and Thy paths are in many waters; and Thy footsteps shall not be known."[5]

8. All this, speaking spiritually, is to be understood in the sense wherein we are speaking. For the illumination of the round earth by the lightnings of God is the enlightenment which is produced by this Divine contemplation in the faculties of the soul; the moving and trembling of the earth is the painful purgation which is caused therein; and to say that the way and the road of God whereby the soul journeys to Him is in the sea, and His footprints are in many waters and for this reason shall not be known, is as much as to say that this road whereby the soul journeys to God is as secret and as hidden from the sense of the soul as the way of one that walks on the sea, whose paths and footprints are not known, is hidden from the sense of the body. The steps and footprints which God is imprinting upon the souls that He desires to bring near to Himself, and to make great in union with His Wisdom, have also this property, that they are not known. Wherefore in the Book of Job mention is made of this matter, in these words: "Hast thou perchance known the paths of the great clouds or the perfect knowledges?"[6] By this are understood the ways and roads whereby God continually exalts souls and perfects them in His Wisdom, which souls are here understood by the clouds. It follows, then, that this contemplation which is guiding the soul to God is secret wisdom.

CHAPTER XVIII

Explains how this secret wisdom is likewise a ladder.

IT NOW remains to consider the second point—namely, how this secret wisdom is likewise a ladder. With respect to this it must be known that we can call this secret contemplation a ladder for many reasons. In the first place, because, just as men mount by means of ladders and climb

---

[4] Baruch iii, 31.
[5] Psalm lxxvii, 18–19.
[6] Job xxxvii, 16.

up to possessions and treasures and things that are in strong places, even so also, by means of this secret contemplation, without knowing how, the soul ascends and climbs up to a knowledge and possession of the good things and treasures of Heaven. This is well expressed by the royal prophet David, when he says: "Blessed is he that hath Thy favor and help, for such a man hath placed in his heart ascensions into the vale of tears in the place which he hath appointed; for after this manner the Lord of the law shall give blessing, and they shall go from virtue to virtue as from step to step, and the God of gods shall be seen in Sion."[1] This God is the treasure of the strong place of Sion, which is happiness.

2. We may also call it a ladder because, even as the ladder has those same steps in order that men may mount, it has them also that they may descend; even so is it likewise with this secret contemplation, for those same communications which it causes in the soul raise it up to God, yet humble it with respect to itself. For communications which are indeed of God have this property, that they humble the soul and at the same time exalt it. For, upon this road, to go down is to go up, and to go up, to go down, for he that humbles himself is exalted and he that exalts himself is humbled.[2] And besides the fact that the virtue of humility is greatness, for the exercise of the soul therein, God is wont to make it mount by this ladder so that it may descend, and to make it descend so that it may mount, that the words of the Wise Man may thus be fulfilled, namely: "Before the soul is exalted, it is humbled; and before it is humbled, it is exalted."[3]

3. Speaking now in a natural way, the soul that desires to consider it will be able to see how on this road (we leave apart the spiritual aspect, of which the soul is not conscious) it has to suffer many ups and downs, and how the prosperity which it enjoys is followed immediately by certain storms and trials; so much so, that it appears to have been given that period of calm in order that it might be forewarned and strengthened against the poverty which has followed; just as after misery and torment there come abundance and calm. It seems to the soul as if, before celebrating that festival, it has first been made to keep that vigil. This is the ordinary course and proceeding of the state of contemplation until the soul arrives at the state of quietness; it never remains in the same state for long together, but is ascending and descending continually.

4. The reason for this is that, as the state of perfection, which consists in the perfect love of God and contempt for self, cannot exist unless it have these two parts, which are the knowledge of God and of oneself, the soul has of necessity to be practiced first in the one and then in the other, now

---

[1] Psalm lxxxiv, 7.
[2] St. Luke xiv, 11.
[3] Proverbs xviii, 12.

being given to taste of the one—that is, exaltation—and now being made
to experience the other—that is, humiliation—until it has acquired perfect
habits; and then this ascending and descending will cease, since the soul
will have attained to God and become united with Him, which comes to
pass at the summit of this ladder, for the ladder rests and leans upon Him.
For this ladder of contemplation, which, as we have said, comes down
from God, is prefigured by that ladder which Jacob saw as he slept,
whereon angels were ascending and descending, from God to man, and
from man to God, Who Himself was leaning upon the end of the ladder.[4]
All this, says Divine Scripture, took place by night, when Jacob slept, in
order to express how secret is this road and ascent to God, and how different from that of man's knowledge. This is very evident, since ordinarily that
which is of the greatest profit in it—namely, to be ever losing oneself and
becoming as nothing—is considered the worst thing possible; and that
which is of least worth, which is for a soul to find consolation and sweetness (wherein it ordinarily loses rather than gains), is considered best.

5. But, speaking now somewhat more substantially and properly of this
ladder of secret contemplation, we shall observe that the principal characteristic of contemplation, on account of which it is here called a ladder,
is that it is the science of love. This, as we have said, is an infused and loving knowledge of God, which enlightens the soul and at the same time
enkindles it with love, until it is raised up step by step, even unto God its
Creator. For it is love alone that unites and joins the soul with God. To the
end that this may be seen more clearly, we shall here indicate the steps of
this Divine ladder one by one, pointing out briefly the marks and effects
of each, so that the soul may conjecture hereby on which of them it is
standing. We shall therefore distinguish them by their effects, as do Saint
Bernard and Saint Thomas, for to know them in themselves is not possible after a natural manner, inasmuch as this ladder of love is, as we have
said, so secret that God alone is He that measures and weighs it.

CHAPTER XIX

*Begins to explain the ten steps of the mystic ladder of Divine love, accord-
ing to Saint Bernard and Saint Thomas. The first five are here treated.*

WE OBSERVE, then, that the steps of this ladder of love by which the soul
mounts, then, one by one, to God, are ten. The first step of love causes
the soul to languish, and this to its advantage. The Bride is speaking

---

[4] Genesis xxviii, 12.

from this step of love when she says: "I adjure you, daughters of Jerusalem, that, if ye find my Beloved, ye tell Him that I am sick with love."[1] This sickness, however, is not unto death, but for the glory of God, for in this sickness the soul swoons as to sin and as to all things that are not God, for the sake of God Himself, even as David testifies, saying: "My soul hath swooned away"[2]—that is, with respect to all things, for Thy salvation. For just as a sick man first of all loses his appetite and taste for all food, and his color changes, so likewise in this degree of love the soul loses its taste and desire for all things and changes its color and the other accidentals of its past life, like one in love. The soul falls not into this sickness if excess of heat be not communicated to it from above, even as is expressed in that verse of David which says: *Pluviam voluntariam segregabis, Deus, hæreditati tuæ, et infirmata est,*[3] etc. This sickness and swooning to all things, which is the beginning and the first step on the road to God, we clearly described above, when we were speaking of the annihilation wherein the soul finds itself when it begins to climb this ladder of contemplative purgation, when it can find no pleasure, support, consolation or abiding-place in anything soever. Wherefore from this step it begins at once to climb to the second.

2. The second step causes the soul to seek God without ceasing. Wherefore, when the Bride says that she sought Him by night upon her bed (when she had swooned away according to the first step of love) and found Him not, she said: "I will arise and will seek Him Whom my soul loveth."[4] This, as we say, the soul does without ceasing, as David counsels it, saying: "Seek ye ever the face of God, and seek ye Him in all things, tarrying not until ye find Him";[5] like the Bride, who, having enquired for Him of the watchmen, passed on at once and left them. Mary Magdalene did not even notice the angels at the sepulchre.[6] On this step the soul now walks so anxiously that it seeks the Beloved in all things. In whatsoever it thinks, it thinks at once of the Beloved. Of whatsoever it speaks, in whatsoever matters present themselves, it is speaking and communing at once with the Beloved. When it eats, when it sleeps, when it watches, when it does aught soever, all its care is about the Beloved, as is said above with respect to the yearnings of love. And now, as love begins to recover its health and find new strength in the love of this second step, it begins at once to mount to the third, by means of a certain degree of new purgation in the night, as we shall afterwards describe, which produces in the soul the following effects.

---

[1] Canticles v, 8.
[2] Psalm cxliii, 7.
[3] Psalm lxviii, 9.
[4] Canticles iii, 2.
[5] Psalm cv, 4.
[6] St. John, xx.

3. The third step of the ladder of love is that which causes the soul to work and gives it fervor so that it fails not. Concerning this the royal Prophet says: "Blessed is the man that feareth the Lord, for in His commandments he is eager to labor greatly."[7] Wherefore if fear, being the son of love, causes within him this eagerness to labor, what will be done by love itself? On this step the soul considers great works undertaken for the Beloved as small; many things as few; and the long time for which it serves Him as short, by reason of the fire of love wherein it is now burning. Even so to Jacob, though after seven years he had been made to serve seven more, they seemed few because of the greatness of his love.[8] Now if the love of a mere creature could accomplish so much in Jacob, what will love of the Creator be able to do when on this third step it takes possession of the soul? Here, for the great love which the soul bears to God, it suffers great pains and afflictions because of the little that it does for God; and if it were lawful for it to be destroyed a thousand times for Him it would be comforted. Wherefore it considers itself useless in all that it does and thinks itself to be living in vain. Another wondrous effect produced here in the soul is that it considers itself as being, most certainly, worse than all other souls: first, because love is continually teaching it how much is due to God; and second, because, as the works which it here does for God are many and it knows them all to be faulty and imperfect, they all bring it confusion and affliction, for it realizes in how lowly a manner it is working for God, Who is so high. On this third step, the soul is very far from vainglory or presumption, and from condemning others. These anxious effects, with many others like them, are produced in the soul by this third step; wherefore it gains courage and strength from them in order to mount to the fourth step, which is that that follows.

4. The fourth step of this ladder of love is that whereby there is caused in the soul an habitual suffering because of the Beloved, yet without weariness. For, as Saint Augustine says, love makes all things that are great, grievous and burdensome to be almost naught. From this step the Bride was speaking when, desiring to attain to the last step, she said to the Spouse: "Set me as a seal upon thy heart, as a seal upon thine arm; for love—that is, the act and work of love—is strong as death, and emulation and importunity last as long as hell."[9] The spirit here has so much strength that it has subjected the flesh and takes as little account of it as does the tree of one of its leaves. In no way does

---

[7] Psalm cxii, 1.
[8] Genesis xxix, 20.
[9] Canticles viii, 5.

the soul here seek its own consolation or pleasure, either in God, or in aught else, nor does it desire or seek to pray to God for favors, for it sees clearly that it has already received enough of these, and all its anxiety is set upon the manner wherein it will be able to do something that is pleasing to God and to render Him some service such as He merits and in return for what it has received from Him, although it be greatly to its cost. The soul says in its heart and spirit: Ah, my God and Lord! How many are there that go to seek in Thee their own consolation and pleasure, and desire Thee to grant them favors and gifts; but those who long to do Thee pleasure and to give Thee something at their cost, setting their own interests last, are very few. The failure, my God, is not in Thy unwillingness to grant us new favors, but in our neglect to use those that we have received in Thy service alone, in order to constrain Thee to grant them to us continually. Exceeding lofty is this step of love; for, as the soul goes ever after God with love so true, imbued with the spirit of suffering for His sake, His Majesty oftentimes and quite habitually grants it joy, and visits it sweetly and delectably in the spirit; for the boundless love of Christ, the Word, cannot suffer the afflictions of His lover without succoring him. This He affirmed through Jeremias, saying: "I have remembered thee, pitying thy youth and tenderness, when thou wentest after Me in the wilderness."[10] Speaking spiritually, this denotes the detachment which the soul now has interiorly from every creature, so that it rests not and nowhere finds quietness. This fourth step enkindles the soul and makes it to burn in such desire for God that it causes it to mount to the fifth, which is that which follows.

5. The fifth step of this ladder of love makes the soul to desire and long for God impatiently. On this step the vehemence of the lover to comprehend the Beloved and be united with Him is such that every delay, however brief, becomes very long, wearisome and oppressive to it, and it continually believes itself to be finding the Beloved. And when it sees its desire frustrated (which is at almost every moment), it swoons away with its yearning, as says the Psalmist, speaking from this step, in these words: "My soul longs and faints for the dwellings of the Lord."[11] On this step the lover must needs see that which he loves, or die; at this step was Rachel, when, for the great longing that she had for children, she said to Jacob, her spouse: "Give me children, else shall I die."[12] Here men suffer hunger like dogs and go about and surround the city

[10] Jeremias ii, 2.
[11] Psalm lxxxiv, 2.
[12] Genesis xxx, 1.

of God. On this step, which is one of hunger, the soul is nourished upon love; for, even as is its hunger, so is its abundance; so that it rises hence to the sixth step, producing the effects which follow.

CHAPTER XX

Wherein are treated the other five steps of love.

ON THE sixth step the soul runs swiftly to God and touches Him again and again; and it runs without fainting by reason of its hope. For here the love that has made it strong makes it to fly swiftly. Of this step the prophet Isaias speaks thus: "The saints that hope in God shall renew their strength; they shall take wings as the eagle; they shall fly and shall not faint,"[1] as they did at the fifth step. To this step likewise alludes that verse of the Psalm: "As the hart desires the waters, my soul desires Thee, O God."[2] For the hart, in its thirst, runs to the waters with great swiftness. The cause of this swiftness in love which the soul has on this step is that its charity is greatly enlarged within it, since the soul is here almost wholly purified, as is said likewise in the Psalm, namely: *Sine iniquitate cucurri.*[3] And in another Psalm: "I ran the way of Thy commandments when Thou didst enlarge my heart";[4] and thus from this sixth step the soul at once mounts to the seventh, which is that which follows.

2. The seventh step of this ladder makes the soul to become vehement in its boldness. Here love employs not its judgment in order to hope, nor does it take counsel so that it may draw back, neither can any shame restrain it; for the favor which God here grants to the soul causes it to become vehement in its boldness. Hence follows that which the Apostle says, namely: That charity believeth all things, hopeth all things and is capable of all things.[5] Of this step spake Moses, when he entreated God to pardon the people, and if not, to blot out his name from the book of life wherein He had written it.[6] Men like these obtain from God that which they beg of Him with desire. Wherefore David says: "Delight thou in God and He will give thee the petitions of thy

---

[1] Isaias xl, 31.
[2] Psalm xlii, 1.
[3] Psalm lix, 4.
[4] Psalm cxix, 32.
[5] 1 Corinthians xiii, 7.
[6] Exodus xxxii, 31–2.

heart."[7] On this step the Bride grew bold, and said: *Osculetur me osculo oris sui.*[8] To this step it is not lawful for the soul to aspire boldly, unless it feel the interior favor of the King's sceptre extended to it, lest perchance it fall from the other steps which it has mounted up to this point, and wherein it must ever possess itself in humility. From this daring and power which God grants to the soul on this seventh step, so that it may be bold with God in the vehemence of love, follows the eighth, which is that wherein it takes the Beloved captive and is united with Him, as follows.

3. The eighth step of love causes the soul to seize Him and hold Him fast without letting Him go, even as the Bride says, after this manner: "I found Him Whom my heart and soul love; I held Him and I will not let Him go."[9] On this step of union the soul satisfies her desire, but not continuously. Certain souls climb some way, and then lose their hold; for, if this state were to continue, it would be glory itself in this life; and thus the soul remains therein for very short periods of time. To the prophet Daniel, because he was a man of desires, was sent a command from God to remain on this step, when it was said to him: "Daniel, stay upon thy step, because thou art a man of desires."[10] After this step follows the ninth, which is that of souls now perfect, as we shall afterwards say, which is that that follows.

4. The ninth step of love makes the soul to burn with sweetness. This step is that of the perfect, who now burn sweetly in God. For this sweet and delectable ardour is caused in them by the Holy Spirit by reason of the union which they have with God. For this cause Saint Gregory says, concerning the Apostles, that when the Holy Spirit came upon them visibly they burned inwardly and sweetly through love. Of the good things and riches of God which the soul enjoys on this step, we cannot speak; for if many books were to be written concerning it the greater part would still remain untold. For this cause, and because we shall say something of it hereafter, I say no more here than that after this follows the tenth and last step of this ladder of love, which belongs not to this life.

5. The tenth and last step of this secret ladder of love causes the soul to become wholly assimilated to God, by reason of the clear and immediate vision of God which it then possesses; when, having ascended in

---

[7] Psalm xxxvii, 4.
[8] Canticles i, 1.
[9] Canticles iii, 4.
[10] Daniel x, 11.

this life to the ninth step, it goes forth from the flesh. These souls, who are few, enter not into purgatory, since they have already been wholly purged by love. Of these Saint Matthew says: *Beati mundo corde: quoniam ipsi Deum videbunt.*[11] And, as we say, this vision is the cause of the perfect likeness of the soul to God, for, as Saint John says, we know that we shall be like Him.[12] Not because the soul will come to have the capacity of God, for that is impossible; but because all that it is will become like to God, for which cause it will be called, and will be, God by participation.

6. This is the secret ladder whereof the soul here speaks, although upon these higher steps it is no longer very secret to the soul, since much is revealed to it by love, through the great effects which love produces in it. But, on this last step of clear vision, which is the last step of the ladder whereon God leans, as we have said already, there is naught that is hidden from the soul, by reason of its complete assimilation. Wherefore Our Saviour says: "In that day ye shall ask Me nothing," etc.[13] But, until that day, however high a point the soul may reach, there remains something hidden from it—namely, all that it lacks for total assimilation in the Divine Essence. After this manner, by this mystical theology and secret love, the soul continues to rise above all things and above itself, and to mount upward to God. For love is like fire, which ever rises upward with the desire to be absorbed in the centre of its sphere.

CHAPTER XXI

Which explains the word "disguised," and describes the colors of the disguise of the soul in this night.

NOW THAT we have explained the reasons why the soul called this contemplation a "secret ladder," it remains for us to explain likewise the word "disguised," and the reason why the soul says also that it went forth by this "secret ladder" in "disguise."

2. For the understanding of this it must be known that to disguise oneself is naught else but to hide and cover oneself beneath another garb and figure than one's own—sometimes in order to show forth, under that garb

---

[11] St. Matthew v, 8.
[12] 1 John iii, 2.
[13] St. John xvi, 23.

or figure, the will and purpose which is in the heart to gain the grace and will of one who is greatly loved; sometimes, again, to hide oneself from one's rivals and thus to accomplish one's object better. At such times a man assumes the garments and livery which best represent and indicate the affection of his heart and which best conceal him from his rivals.

3. The soul, then, touched with the love of Christ the Spouse, and longing to attain to His grace and gain His goodwill, goes forth here disguised with that disguise which most vividly represents the affections of its spirit and which will protect it most securely on its journey from its adversaries and enemies, which are the devil, the world and the flesh. Thus the livery which it wears is of three chief colors—white, green and purple—denoting the three theological virtues, faith, hope and charity. By these the soul will not only gain the grace and goodwill of its Beloved, but it will travel in security and complete protection from its three enemies: for faith is an inward tunic of a whiteness so pure that it completely dazzles the eyes of the understanding. And thus, when the soul journeys in its vestment of faith, the devil can neither see it nor succeed in harming it, since it is well protected by faith—more so than by all the other virtues—against the devil, who is at once the strongest and the most cunning of enemies.

4. It is clear that Saint Peter could find no better protection than faith to save him from the devil, when he said: *Cui resistite fortes in fide.*[1] And in order to gain the grace of the Beloved, and union with Him, the soul cannot put on a better vest and tunic, to serve as a foundation and beginning of the other vestments of the virtues, than this white garment of faith, for without it, as the Apostle says, it is impossible to please God, and with it, it is impossible to fail to please Him. For He Himself says through a prophet: *Sponsabo te mihi in fide.*[2] Which is as much as to say: If thou desirest, O soul, to be united and betrothed to Me, thou must come inwardly clad in faith.

5. This white garment of faith was worn by the soul on its going forth from this dark night, when, walking in interior constraint and darkness, as we have said before, it received no aid, in the form of light, from its understanding, neither from above, since Heaven seemed to be closed to it and God hidden from it, nor from below, since those that taught it satisfied it not. It suffered with constancy and persevered, passing through those trials without fainting or failing the Beloved, Who in trials and tribulations

[1] 1 Peter v, 9.
[2] Osee ii, 20.

proves the faith of His Bride, so that afterwards she may truly repeat this saying of David, namely: "By the words of Thy lips I kept hard ways."[3]

6. Next, over this white tunic of faith the soul now puts on the second color, which is a green vestment. By this, as we said, is signified the virtue of hope, wherewith, as in the first case, the soul is delivered and protected from the second enemy, which is the world. For this green color of living hope in God gives the soul such ardour and courage and aspiration to the things of eternal life that, by comparison with what it hopes for therein, all things of the world seem to it to be, as in truth they are, dry and faded and dead and nothing worth. The soul now divests and strips itself of all these worldly vestments and garments, setting its heart upon naught that is in the world and hoping for naught, whether of that which is or of that which is to be, but living clad only in the hope of eternal life. Wherefore, when the heart is thus lifted up above the world, not only can the world neither touch the heart nor lay hold on it, but it cannot even come within sight of it.

7. And thus, in this green livery and disguise, the soul journeys in complete security from this second enemy, which is the world. For Saint Paul speaks of hope as the helmet of salvation[4]—that is, a piece of armour that protects the whole head, and covers it so that there remains uncovered only a visor through which it may look. And hope has this property, that it covers all the senses of the head of the soul, so that there is naught soever pertaining to the world in which they can be immersed, nor is there an opening through which any arrow of the world can wound them. It has a visor, however, which the soul is permitted to use so that its eyes may look upward, but nowhere else; for this is the function which hope habitually performs in the soul, namely, the directing of its eyes upwards to look at God alone, even as David declared that his eyes were directed, when he said: *Oculi mei semper ad Dominum.*[5] He hoped for no good thing elsewhere, save as he himself says in another Psalm: "Even as the eyes of the handmaid are set upon the hands of her mistress, even so are our eyes set upon our Lord God, until He have mercy upon us as we hope in Him."[6]

8. For this reason, because of this green livery (since the soul is ever looking to God and sets its eyes on naught else, neither is pleased with aught save with Him alone), the Beloved has such great pleasure with

---

[3] Psalm xvii, 4.
[4] 1 Thessalonians v, 8.
[5] Psalm xxv, 15.
[6] Psalm cxxiii, 2.

the soul that it is true to say that the soul obtains from Him as much as it hopes for from Him. Wherefore the Spouse in the Songs tells the Bride that, by looking upon Him with one eye alone, she has wounded His heart.[7] Without this green livery of hope in God alone it would be impossible for the soul to go forth to encompass this loving achievement, for it would have no success, since that which moves and conquers is the importunity of hope.

9. With this livery of hope the soul journeys in disguise through this secret and dark night whereof we have spoken; for it is so completely voided of every possession and support that it fixes its eyes and its care upon naught but God, putting its mouth in the dust,[8] if so be there may be hope—to repeat the quotation made above from Jeremias.[9]

10. Over the white and the green vestments, as the crown and perfection of this disguise and livery, the soul now puts on the third color, which is a splendid garment of purple. By this is denoted the third virtue, which is charity. This not only adds grace to the other two colors, but causes the soul to rise to so lofty a point that it is brought near to God, and becomes very beautiful and pleasing to Him, so that it makes bold to say: "Albeit I am black, O daughters of Jerusalem, I am comely; wherefore the King hath loved me and hath brought me into His chambers."[10] This livery of charity, which is that of love, and causes greater love in the Beloved, not only protects the soul and hides it from the third enemy, which is the flesh (for where there is true love of God there enters neither love of self nor that of the things of self), but even gives worth to the other virtues, bestowing on them vigour and strength to protect the soul, and grace and beauty to please the Beloved with them, for without charity no virtue has grace before God. This is the purple which is spoken of in the Songs,[11] upon which God reclines. Clad in this purple livery the soul journeys when (as has been explained above in the first stanza) it goes forth from itself in the dark night, and from all things created, "kindled in love with yearnings," by this secret ladder of contemplation, to the perfect union of love of God, its beloved salvation.

11. This, then, is the disguise which the soul says that it wears in the night of faith, upon this secret ladder, and these are its three colors. They constitute a most fit preparation for the union of the soul with God, according to its three faculties, which are understanding, memory and

---

[7] Canticles iv, 9.
[8] Lamentations iii, 29.
[9] [For the quotation, see Bk. II, chap. viii, section 1, above.]
[10] Canticles i.
[11] Canticles iii, 10.

will. For faith voids and darkens the understanding as to all its natural intelligence, and herein prepares it for union with Divine Wisdom. Hope voids and withdraws the memory from all creature possessions; for, as Saint Paul says, hope is for that which is not possessed;[12] and thus it withdraws the memory from that which it is capable of possessing, and sets it on that for which it hopes. And for this cause hope in God alone prepares the memory purely for union with God. Charity, in the same way, voids and annihilates the affections and desires of the will for whatever is not God, and sets them upon Him alone; and thus this virtue prepares this faculty and unites it with God through love. And thus, since the function of these virtues is the withdrawal of the soul from all that is less than God, their function is consequently that of joining it with God.

12. And thus, unless it journeys earnestly, clad in the garments of these three virtues, it is impossible for the soul to attain to the perfection of union with God through love. Wherefore, in order that the soul might attain that which it desired, which was this loving and delectable union with its Beloved, this disguise and clothing which it assumed was most necessary and convenient. And likewise to have succeeded in thus clothing itself and persevering until it should obtain the end and aspiration which it had so much desired, which was the union of love, was a great and happy chance, wherefore in this line the soul also says:

Oh, happy chance!

CHAPTER XXII

Explains the third line of the second stanza.

IT IS very clear that it was a happy chance for this soul to go forth with such an enterprise as this, for it was its going forth that delivered it from the devil and from the world and from its own sensuality, as we have said. Having attained liberty of spirit, so precious and so greatly desired by all, it went forth from low things to high; from terrestrial, it became celestial; from human, Divine. Thus it came to have its conversation in the heavens, as has the soul in this state of perfection, even as we shall go on to say in what follows, although with rather more brevity.

2. For the most important part of my task, and the part which chiefly led me to undertake it, was the explanation of this night to many souls

---

[12] Romans viii, 24.

who pass through it and yet know nothing about it, as was said in the prologue. Now this explanation and exposition has already been half completed. Although much less has been said of it than might be said, we have shown how many are the blessings which the soul bears with it through the night and how happy is the chance whereby it passes through it, so that, when a soul is terrified by the horror of so many trials, it is also encouraged by the certain hope of so many and such precious blessings of God as it gains therein. And furthermore, for yet another reason, this was a happy chance for the soul; and this reason is given in the following line:

In darkness and in concealment.

CHAPTER XXIII

Expounds the fourth line and describes the wondrous hiding-place wherein the soul is set during this night. Shows how, although the devil has an entrance into other places that are very high, he has none into this.

"IN CONCEALMENT" is as much as to say "in a hiding-place," or "in hiding"; and thus, what the soul here says (namely, that it went forth "in darkness and in concealment") is a more complete explanation of the great security which it describes itself in the first line of the stanza as possessing, by means of this dark contemplation upon the road of the union of the love of God.

2. When the soul, then, says "in darkness and in concealment," it means that, inasmuch as it journeyed in darkness after the manner afore-mentioned, it went in hiding and in concealment from the devil and from his wiles and stratagems. The reason why, as it journeys in the darkness of this contemplation, the soul is free, and is hidden from the stratagems of the devil, is that the infused contemplation which it here possesses is infused into it passively and secretly, without the knowledge of the senses and faculties, whether interior or exterior, of the sensual part. And hence it follows that, not only does it journey in hiding, and is free from the impediment which these faculties can set in its way because of its natural weakness, but likewise from the devil; who, except through these faculties of the sensual part, cannot reach or know that which is in the soul, nor that which is taking place within it. Wherefore, the more spiritual, the more interior and the more remote from the senses is the communica-tion, the farther does the devil fall short of understanding it.

3. And thus it is of great importance for the security of the soul that

its inward communication with God should be of such a kind that its very senses of the lower part will remain in darkness and be without knowledge of it, and attain not to it: first, so that it may be possible for the spiritual communication to be more abundant, and that the weakness of its sensual part may not hinder the liberty of its spirit; secondly because, as we say, the soul journeys more securely since the devil cannot penetrate so far. In this way we may understand that passage where Our Saviour, speaking in a spiritual sense, says: "Let not thy left hand know what thy right hand doeth."[1] Which is as though He had said: Let not thy left hand know that which takes place upon thy right hand, which is the higher and spiritual part of the soul; that is, let it be of such a kind that the lower portion of thy soul, which is the sensual part, may not attain to it; let it be a secret between the spirit and God alone.

4. It is quite true that oftentimes, when these very intimate and secret spiritual communications are present and take place in the soul, although the devil cannot get to know of what kind and manner they are, yet the great repose and silence which some of them cause in the senses and the faculties of the sensual part make it clear to him that they are taking place and that the soul is receiving a certain blessing from them. And then, as he sees that he cannot succeed in thwarting them in the depth of the soul, he does what he can to disturb and disquiet the sensual part—that part to which he is able to attain—now by means of afflictions, now by terrors and fears, with intent to disquiet and disturb the higher and spiritual part of the soul by this means, with respect to that blessing which it then receives and enjoys. But often, when the communication of such contemplation makes its naked assault upon the soul and exerts its strength upon it, the devil, with all his diligence, is unable to disturb it; rather the soul receives a new and a greater advantage and a securer peace. For, when it feels the disturbing presence of the enemy, then—wondrous thing!—without knowing how it comes to pass, and without any efforts of its own, it enters farther into its own interior depths, feeling that it is indeed being set in a sure refuge, where it perceives itself to be most completely withdrawn and hidden from the enemy. And thus its peace and joy, which the devil is attempting to take from it, are increased; and all the fear that assails it remains without; and it becomes clearly and exultingly conscious of its secure enjoyment of that quiet peace and sweetness of the hidden Spouse, which neither the world nor the devil can give it or take from it. In that state, therefore, it realizes the truth of the words of the Bride about this, in the Songs, namely: "See how threescore strong men surround the bed of Solomon, etc., because of the fears of the night."[2] It

---

[1] St. Matthew vi, 3.
[2] Canticles iii, 7–8.

is conscious of this strength and peace, although it is often equally conscious that its flesh and bones are being tormented from without.

5. At other times, when the spiritual communication is not made in any great measure to the spirit, but the senses have a part therein, the devil more easily succeeds in disturbing the spirit and raising a tumult within it, by means of the senses, with these terrors. Great are the torment and the affliction which are then caused in the spirit; at times they exceed all that can be expressed. For, when there is a naked contact of spirit with spirit, the horror is intolerable which the evil spirit causes in the good spirit (I mean, in the soul), when its tumult reaches it. This is expressed likewise by the Bride in the Songs, when she says that it has happened thus to her at a time when she wished to descend to interior recollection in order to have fruition of these blessings. She says: "I went down into the garden of nuts to see the apples of the valleys, and if the vine had flourished. I knew not; my soul troubled me because of the chariots"—that is, because of the chariots and the noise of Aminadab, which is the devil.[3]

6. At other times it comes to pass that the devil is occasionally able to see certain favors which God is pleased to grant the soul when they are bestowed upon it by the mediation of a good angel; for of those favors which come through a good angel God habitually allows the enemy to have knowledge: partly so that he may do that which he can against them according to the measure of justice, and that thus he may not be able to allege with truth that no opportunity is given him for conquering the soul, as he said concerning Job.[4] This would be the case if God allowed not a certain equality between the two warriors—namely, the good angel and the bad—when they strive for the soul, so that the victory of either may be of the greater worth, and the soul that is victorious and faithful in temptation may be the more abundantly rewarded.

7. We must observe, therefore, that it is for this reason that, in proportion as God is guiding the soul and communing with it, He gives the devil leave to act with it after this manner. When the soul has genuine visions by the instrumentality of the good angel (for it is by this instrumentality that they habitually come, even though Christ reveal Himself, for He scarcely ever appears in His actual person), God also gives the wicked angel leave to present to the soul false visions of this very type in such a way that the soul which is not cautious may easily be deceived by their outward appearance, as many souls have been. Of

---

[3] Canticles vi, 11–12.
[4] Job i, 1–11.

this there is a figure in Exodus,[5] where it is said that all the genuine
signs that Moses wrought were wrought likewise in appearance by the
magicians of Pharao. If he brought forth frogs, they brought them forth
likewise; if he turned water into blood, they did the same.

8. And not only does the evil one imitate God in this type of bodily
vision, but he also imitates and interferes in spiritual communications
which come through the instrumentality of an angel, when he succeeds in seeing them, as we say (for, as Job said: *Omne sublime videt*[6]).
These, however, as they are without form and figure (for it is the nature
of spirit to have no such thing), he cannot imitate and counterfeit like
those others which are presented under some species or figure. And
thus, in order to attack the soul, in the same way as that wherein it is
being visited, his fearful spirit presents a similar vision in order to attack
and destroy spiritual things by spiritual. When this comes to pass just as
the good angel is about to communicate spiritual contemplation to
the soul, it is impossible for the soul to shelter itself in the secrecy
and hiding-place of contemplation with sufficient rapidity not to be
observed by the devil; and thus he appears to it and produces a certain
horror and perturbation of spirit which at times is most distressing to
the soul. Sometimes the soul can speedily free itself from him, so that
there is no opportunity for the aforementioned horror of the evil spirit
to make an impression on it; and it becomes recollected within itself,
being favored, to this end, by the effectual spiritual grace that the good
angel then communicates to it.

9. At other times the devil prevails and encompasses the soul with a
perturbation and horror which is a greater affliction to it than any torment in this life could be. For, as this horrible communication passes
direct from spirit to spirit, in something like nakedness and clearly dis-
tinguished from all that is corporeal, it is grievous beyond what every
sense can feel; and this lasts in the spirit for some time, yet not for long,
for otherwise the spirit would be driven forth from the flesh by the
vehement communication of the other spirit. Afterwards there remains
to it the memory thereof, which is sufficient to cause it great affliction.

10. All that we have here described comes to pass in the soul passively,
without its doing or undoing anything of itself with respect to it. But in
this connection it must be known that, when the good angel permits
the devil to gain this advantage of assailing the soul with this spiritual
horror, he does it to purify the soul and to prepare it by means of this
spiritual vigil for some great spiritual favor and festival which he desires
to grant it, for he never mortifies save to give life, nor humbles save to

---

[5] Exodus vii, 11–22; viii, 7.
[6] Job xli, 25.

exalt, which comes to pass shortly afterwards. Then, according as was the dark and horrible purgation which the soul suffered, so is the fruition now granted it of a wondrous and delectable spiritual contemplation, sometimes so lofty that there is no language to describe it. But the spirit has been greatly refined by the preceding horror of the evil spirit, in order that it may be able to receive this blessing; for these spiritual visions belong to the next life rather than to this, and when one of them is seen this is a preparation for the next.

11. This is to be understood with respect to occasions when God visits the soul by the instrumentality of a good angel, wherein, as has been said, the soul is not so totally in darkness and in concealment that the enemy cannot come within reach of it. But, when God Himself visits it, then the words of this line are indeed fulfilled, and it is in total darkness and in concealment from the enemy that the soul receives these spiritual favors of God. The reason for this is that, as His Majesty dwells substantially in the soul, where neither angel nor devil can attain to an understanding of that which comes to pass, they cannot know the intimate and secret communications which take place there between the soul and God. These communications, since the Lord Himself works them, are wholly Divine and sovereign, for they are all substantial touches of Divine union between the soul and God; in one of which the soul receives a greater blessing than in all the rest, since this is the loftiest degree of prayer in existence.

12. For these are the touches that the Bride entreated of Him in the Songs, saying: *Osculetur me osculo oris sui*.[7] Since this is a thing which takes place in such close intimacy with God, whereto the soul desires with such yearnings to attain, it esteems and longs for a touch of this Divinity more than all the other favors that God grants it. Wherefore, after many such favors have been granted to the Bride in the said Songs, of which she has sung therein, she is not satisfied, but entreats Him for these Divine touches, saying: "Who shall give Thee to me, my brother, that I might find Thee alone without, sucking the breasts of my mother, so that I might kiss Thee with the mouth of my soul, and that thus no man should despise me or make bold to attack me."[8] By this she denotes the communication which God Himself alone makes to her, as we are saying, far from all the creatures and without their knowledge, for this is meant by "alone and without, sucking, etc." — that is, drying up and draining the breasts of the desires and affections of the sensual part of the soul. This takes place when the soul, in intimate peace and delight, has fruition of these blessings, with liberty of

---

[7] Canticles i, 1.
[8] Canticles viii, 1.

spirit, and without the sensual part being able to hinder it, or the devil to thwart it by means thereof. And then the devil would not make bold to attack it, for he would not reach it, neither could he attain to an understanding of these Divine touches in the substance of the soul in the loving substance of God.

13. To this blessing none attains save through intimate purgation and detachment and spiritual concealment from all that is creature; it comes to pass in the darkness, as we have already explained at length and as we say with respect to this line. The soul is in concealment and in hiding, in the which hiding-place, as we have now said, it continues to be strengthened in union with God through love, wherefore it sings this in the same phrase, saying: "In darkness and in concealment."

14. When it comes to pass that those favors are granted to the soul in concealment (that is, as we have said, in spirit only), the soul is wont, during some of them, and without knowing how this comes to pass, to see itself so far withdrawn and separated according to the higher and spiritual part, from the sensual and lower portion, that it recognizes in itself two parts so distinct from each other that it believes that the one has naught to do with the other, but that the one is very remote and far withdrawn from the other. And in reality, in a certain way, this is so; for the operation is now wholly spiritual, and the soul receives no communication in its sensual part. In this way the soul gradually becomes wholly spiritual; and in this hiding-place of unitive contemplation its spiritual desires and passions are to a great degree removed and purged away. And thus, speaking of its higher part, the soul then says in this last line:

My house being now at rest.

CHAPTER XXIV

Completes the explanation of the second stanza.

THIS IS as much as to say: The higher portion of my soul being like the lower part also, at rest with respect to its desires and faculties, I went forth to the Divine union of the love of God.

2. Inasmuch as, by means of that war of the dark night, as has been said, the soul is combated and purged after two manners—namely, according to its sensual and its spiritual part—with its senses, faculties and passions, so likewise after two manners—namely, according to these two parts, the sensual and the spiritual—with all its faculties and desires, the soul attains to an enjoyment of peace and rest. For this reason, as has

likewise been said, the soul twice pronounces this line—namely, in this stanza and in the last—because of these two portions of the soul, the spiritual and the sensual, which, in order that they may go forth to the Divine union of love, must needs first be reformed, ordered and tranquilized with respect to the sensual and to the spiritual, according to the nature of the state of innocence which was Adam's.[1] And thus this line which, in the first stanza, was understood of the repose of the lower and sensual portion, is, in this second stanza, understood more particularly of the higher and spiritual part; for which reason it is repeated.

3. This repose and quiet of this spiritual house the soul comes to attain, habitually and perfectly (in so far as the condition of this life allows), by means of the acts of the substantial touches of Divine union whereof we have just spoken; which, in concealment, and hidden from the perturbation of the devil, and of its own senses and passions, the soul has been receiving from the Divinity, wherein it has been purifying itself, as I say, resting, strengthening and confirming itself in order to be able to receive the said union once and for all, which is the Divine betrothal between the soul and the Son of God. As soon as these two houses of the soul have together become tranquilized and strengthened, with all their domestics—namely, the faculties and desires—and have put these domestics to sleep and made them to be silent with respect to all things, both above and below, this Divine Wisdom immediately unites itself with the soul by making a new bond of loving possession, and there is fulfilled that which is written in the Book of Wisdom, in these words: *Dum quietum silentium contineret omnia, et nox in suo cursu medium iter haberet, omnipotens sermo tuus Domine a regalibus sedibus.*[2] The same thing is described by the Bride in the Songs,[3] where she says that, after she had passed by those who stripped her of her mantle by night and wounded her, she found Him Whom her soul loved.

4. The soul cannot come to this union without great purity, and this purity is not gained without great detachment from every created thing

---

[1] The Saint's meaing is that for the mystical union of the soul with God such purity and tranquillity of senses and faculties are needful that his condition resembles that state of innocence in which Adam was created, but without the attribute of impeccability, which does not necessarily accompany union, nor can be attained by any, save by a most special privilege of God. Cf. St. Teresa's *Interior Castle*, VII, ii. St. Teresa will be found occasionally to explain points of mystical doctrine which St. John of the Cross takes as being understood.

[2] Wisdom xviii, 14.

[3] Canticles v, 7.

and sharp mortification. This is signified by the stripping of the Bride of her mantle and by her being wounded by night as she sought and went after the Spouse; for the new mantle which belonged to the betrothal could not be put on until the old mantle was stripped off. Wherefore, he that refuses to go forth in the night aforementioned to seek the Beloved, and to be stripped of his own will and to be mortified, but seeks Him upon his bed and at his own convenience, as did the Bride,[4] will not succeed in finding Him. For this soul says of itself that it found Him by going forth in the dark and with yearnings of love.

CHAPTER XXV

Wherein is expounded the third stanza.

In the happy night,   In secret, when none saw me,
Nor I beheld aught,   Without light or guide, save that which burned
  in my heart.

EXPOSITION

THE SOUL still continues the metaphor and similitude of temporal night in describing this its spiritual night, and continues to sing and extol the good properties which belong to it, and which in passing through this night it found and used, to the end that it might attain its desired goal with speed and security. Of these properties it here sets down three.

2. The first, it says, is that in this happy night of contemplation God leads the soul by a manner of contemplation so solitary and secret, so remote and far distant from sense, that naught pertaining to it, nor any touch of created things, succeeds in approaching the soul in such a way as to disturb it and detain it on the road of the union of love.

3. The second property whereof it speaks pertains to the spiritual darkness of this night, wherein all the faculties of the higher part of the soul are in darkness. The soul sees naught, neither looks at aught neither stays in aught that is not God, to the end that it may reach Him, inasmuch as it journeys unimpeded by obstacles of forms and figures, and of natural apprehensions, which are those that are wont to hinder the soul from uniting with the eternal Being of God.

---

[4] Canticles iii, 1.

4. The third is that, although as it journeys it is supported by no particular interior light of understanding, nor by any exterior guide, that it
may receive satisfaction therefrom on this lofty road—it is completely
deprived of all this by this thick darkness—yet its love alone, which
burns at this time, and makes its heart to long for the Beloved, is that
which now moves and guides it, and makes it to soar upward to its God
along the road of solitude, without its knowing how or in what manner.

There follows the line:

In the happy night.[1]

---

[1] Thus end the majority of the MSS. The MSS. say nothing of the incomplete state of
this treatise except that in the Alba de Tormes MS. we read: "Thus far wrote the holy
Fray John of the Cross concerning the purgative way, wherein he treats of the active
and the passive [aspect] of it as is seen in the treatise of the *Ascent of the Mount* and
in this of the *Dark Night,* and, as he died, he wrote no more. And hereafter follows the
illuminative way, and then the unitive." Elsewhere we have said that the lack of any
commentary on the last five stanzas is not due to the Saint's death, since he lived for
many years after writing the commentary on the earlier stanzas.